Clinician's Guide To Nuclear Medicine

Nuclear Cardiology

Dudley J Pennell, MA MB MD MRCP
Senior Lecturer and Honorary Consultant in
Cardiac Imaging. Royal Brompton Hospital,
Sydney Street, London SW3 6NP, UK

Elizabeth Prvulovich, MB MD MRCP
Senior Registrar, Institute of Nuclear Medicine,
University College London School of Medicine,
London W1N 8AA, UK

i

First published/Edition 1995

ISBN 0-901259-10-1

Presented with the compliments of
Amersham International plc
as a service to medical education.

⁄⁄Amersham **HEALTHCARE**

Preface

On behalf of the British Nuclear Medicine Society (BNMS) we began editing a series of books entitled "A Clinician's Guide to Nuclear Medicine" which intends to present the clinical utility of nuclear medicine to all doctors, whether in general medicine, surgical or specialised disciplines. The first three books in this series were published in 1991 and addressed the topics of brain blood flow in neurology and psychiatry, gastroenterology and benign and malignant bone disease.

We are now in a position to publish and complete this series with three further books addressing the topics of cardiology, oncology and nephrourology.

The authors of this specific book on cardiology have over the years shown a specific interest in the application of nuclear medicine and the radioactive tracer principle to clinical cardiology.

It is now proven beyond doubt that nuclear medicine has a major role to play in the diagnosis, follow-up and prognostic assessment of patients with coronary artery disease. It has a supportive role in the investigation of ventricular function and the early detection of regional wall motion abnormalities, and progressively, this activity forms an integral part of the management of patients submitted to treatment regimes which may affect cardiac function.

This book describes in a succinct manner the main areas of application of nuclear medicine to cardiology. It is aimed at the non-expert to increase the awareness and familiarisation of these important management tools in coronary artery disease.

The British Nuclear Medicine Society appreciates a significant grant from Amersham International plc which is making the publication of the three new books in this series possible.

Professor P.J Ell, Series Editor.

ACKNOWLEDGEMENT

The authors would like to thank the following people for their contributions to this book and the development of nuclear cardiology at The Middlesex and Royal Brompton Hospitals:

The staff in both nuclear medicine departments for all their general assistance, all the cardiologists from both sites and referring hospitals for their clinical support and interest (including most notably Howard Swanton, Malcolm Walker, Philip Poole-Wilson, Kim Fox and John Pepper), Richard Underwood for his support and contribution of images, and in particular Peter Ell, whose general contribution to the field of nuclear medicine has been immense, and whose vision and encouragement in the production of this book has been critical.

This book is part of a series sponsored by Amersham International plc for which the authors, editor and the British Nuclear Medicine Society are grateful.

This book is written by enthusiasts to help promote the field of nuclear cardiology, and the editor and the authors (or the British Nuclear Cardiology Group which has a specialist interest, or the British Nuclear Medicine Society) would welcome enquiries for any assistance that may arise.

Produced by Impact Healthcare, part of the Marketing Communication Group Ltd, Hatfield (01707) 273287.
Printed and bound in Great Britain by BPC Wheatons Ltd, Exeter.

Contents

Introduction 1

Myocardial Perfusion Imaging 5

Imaging Techniques 17

Pharmacological Stress Techniques 34

Image Interpretation 56

Diagnosis in Coronary Artery Disease 80

Prognosis in Coronary Artery Disease 95

Bypass Surgery 118

Angioplasty 126

Hibernation 137

Radionuclide Ventriculography 163

Infarct-avid Imaging 189

Positron Emission Tomography 201

Diagnosis in Coronary Artery Disease

NUCLEAR CARDIOLOGY IN THE UK, EUROPE AND THE USA

Nuclear cardiology is established as a major investigative tool,[1,2] but its practice in the United Kingdom is only beginning to gain ground after years of trailing behind Europe and the United States. The rate of myocardial perfusion imaging per thousand of the population per year in the UK has increased from 0.2 in 1988,[3] to 0.3 in 1990,[4] and the most recent estimates currently being compiled by the British Nuclear Cardiology Group suggest a figure of approximately 0.6 for 1993.[5] This has to be compared with considerably higher figures in Europe (in 1992 Belgium 7, Germany 2.9, Austria 2.3 and Holland 2.1, with an overall European average of 1.8)[6] and in the United States (which showed a rate of 3.5 for 1985 that by 1994 had probably doubled). The overall European average for total major nuclear cardiology procedures, including perfusion imaging and ventriculography, is approximately 2.6 per 1000 per year, which compares with 0.9 in the UK. The British Cardiac Society has now indicated that it accepts this European average as the target for provision of nuclear cardiology services in the UK.[7] This implies that a tripling of present activity is required, and this will undoubtedly need better provision of services.

The improvement in the UK has come about from a gradual change in entrenched attitudes regarding exercise electrocardiography and coronary angiography as being the only means by which most patients with coronary artery disease should be managed. The limitations of exercise electrocardiography in the physiological assessment of presence and severity of myocardial ischaemia have been

1

repeatedly exposed, both on a theoretical basis and in clinical practice. At the same time it has become increasingly clear that coronary anatomy alone, as defined by the coronary angiogram, is not capable of defining blood flow at myocardial level (perfusion) because of its limited ability to assess stenoses of intermediate severity, or the combined effect of multiple stenoses, or the degree of protection afforded by collateralisation. Myocardial perfusion imaging as a non–invasive test starts from a different viewpoint and is simply used to assess the *overall* effects of coronary disease irrespective of the actual anatomy.

Myocardial perfusion imaging is also a powerful yet simple approach to the subject of hibernation. Following the introduction of the concept by Rahimtoola in 1985, it is now realised that an important differential diagnosis exists in myocardium with abnormal chronic resting contraction. The downgrading of myocardial contraction may not represent infarction, and revascularisation has been shown to improve regional wall motion, resting ejection fraction, symptoms and prognosis. Such areas are most easily and reliably demonstrated by showing a mismatch between myocardial contraction and the intensity of tracer activity in the same area, which represents the amount of contractile tissue. Whilst other methods such as dobutamine echocardiography and positron emission tomography (FDG imaging) may also be used, their ability to compete with such a clinically robust and inexpensive test as myocardial perfusion imaging remains to be demonstrated.

QUALITY CONTROL AND CLINICAL COLLABORATION

A major issue for nuclear cardiology in the 1990s will be quality control, audit and the investigation of cost-benefit in comparison with other techniques. Reference to this issue is made in the chapter on interpretation of SPET images. Nuclear cardiology will only prosper if high-quality services are routinely available in all the major centres, and preferably this would include all major district general hospitals. This is the recommendation of the British Cardiac Society.[8]

The proper use of clinical feedback and audit in acquisition quality and reporting of studies is vital to maintaining and improving standards, and this needs to be nurtured. National and international programs can help to achieve this end. Collaboration with the referring cardiologist is also vital in developing confidence in the results and gaining an appropriate position for nuclear cardiology in the management of coronary artery disease. Nuclear cardiology practised in a clinical vacuum is likely to be limited, and to generate inappropriate reports. It is therefore vital to bring clinical cardiologists on board ship. Once enthused, experience suggests that most clinical cardiologists readily accept the benefits of nuclear techniques. Training is also vital in order to prepare junior cardiologists for the appropriate use and interpretation of the techniques, and the British Cardiac Society has recommended formal training in nuclear cardiology in the program for higher medical training in cardiovascular medicine.

AIMS OF THIS BOOK

This series of monographs is designed to bring the most important information in the field to the clinician, who understands that the techniques are valuable but who does not have the time to cover the subject in depth in the original literature. For the cardiologist and the nuclear cardiologist, this book is intended to cover the most important practical aspects of image acquisition and interpretation, with a presentation and elucidation of the most salient academic results and arguments from nearly 20 years of experience in nuclear cardiology. Some of the statements within the text are undoubtedly coloured by personal experience and others might have used a different perspective, but within the confines of this short text the aim was to achieve simplicity with a clarity of argument that was not too cluttered with various possibilities. We hope that the cardiological and clinical bias will appeal to clinicians. The text is extensively referenced in the chapters on the most contemporary issues, to allow the more interested reader to refer to original articles.

References

1. Zaret BL, Wackers FJ. Nuclear cardiology. Review article I. *N Engl J Med* 1993; **329**: 775-83.
2. Zaret BL, Wackers FJ. Nuclear cardiology. Review article II. *N Engl J Med* 1993; **329**: 855-63.
3. Underwood SR, Gibson C, Tweddel A, Flint J on behalf of the British Nuclear Cardiology Group. A survey of nuclear cardiological practice in Great Britain. *Br Heart J* 1982; **67**: 273-7.
4. Elliott AT, Shields RA. UK nuclear medicine survey, 1989/90. *Nucl Med Commun* 1993; **14**: 360-4.
5. Pennell DJ, Caplin J, Prvulovich E. British Nuclear Cardiology Group: survey of UK nuclear cardiology practice 1993 (abstract). *Br Heart J* 1995; in press.
6. Personal communication. H Larkin, marketing data 1992, Du Pont pharmaceuticals.
7. Council statement on the demand and need for cardiac services and the development of a waiting list strategy for cardiac disease. British Cardiac Society, London, UK, 1994.
8. A report of a working group of the British Cardiac Society: cardiology in the district general hospital. *Br Heart J* 1994; **72**: 303-8.

Myocardial Perfusion Imaging

RADIOPHARMACEUTICALS

The ideal perfusion tracer

The ideal tracer for the assessment of myocardial perfusion would possess the following properties: distribution in the myocardium in linear proportion to blood flow over the range of values experienced in health and disease, efficient myocardial extraction from the blood on the first passage through the heart, stable retention within the myocardium during data acquisition, rapid elimination allowing repeat studies under different conditions, ready availability, competitive pricing and good imaging characteristics (short half-life, high photon flux, energy between 100 and 200 keV, low radiation burden to the patient). No current tracer possesses all of these properties and compromises have to be made.

THALLIUM-201

Basic properties

Thallium is a metallic element which behaves chemically in a similar manner to potassium, which has a high intracellular concentration, and therefore can be used as a perfusion tracer. ^{201}Tl has been used clinically since the early 1970's for myocardial perfusion studies. In the UK in 1994, it was the most commonly used radiopharmaceutical for cardiac perfusion, although the technetium-99m compounds (MIBI, tetrofosmin) are also widely used.

The principal photon energy of ^{201}Tl is low, and 88% of its emissions are x-rays with photon energies of 60-80 keV. Gamma photons of 135 and 167 keV are also present, but form only 12% of its emissions. Following intravenous injection, approximately 88% is cleared from the blood after the first circulation,[1] but because the blood receives 5% of the cardiac output, only 4% of the total dose is taken up by the myocardium. Uptake into the myocardium peaks at around 10 min after injection. Approximately 60% of the total dose enters the myocyte by active transport via the Na^+/K^+ ATPase pump, and the remaining 40% probably enters passively along the electrochemical gradient. Although acidosis and hypoxaemia have a small effect on ^{201}Tl uptake, this has not been shown to be clinically important, and therefore images of thallium distribution during stress represent heterogeneous blood flow and not ischaemia.[2]

Limitations as an imaging agent

^{201}Tl has a number of undesirable properties which include a low photon energy, a long half-life of 73 h, restricted availability and expense. The low photon energy leads to low-resolution images and significant attenuation by overlying soft tissues. The long half-life means that the size of the administered dose must be restricted in order to minimise the radiation dose to the patient. This, together with the fact that only 4% of the dose is taken up by the myocardium and with the rest taken up mainly by the skeletal muscle and gut, means that the count density of myocardial images is low and that background activity is high. Finally, ^{201}Tl is cyclotron produced and is therefore less readily available and more expensive than generator-produced radioisotopes such as ^{99m}Tc.

Dosimetry

Thallium is given as thallous chloride and the UK Department of Health, ARSAC (Administration of Radioactive Substances Advisory Committee) limit for a single administered dose is 80 MBq. The effective dose equivalent is 0.23 mSv/MBq, yielding a total dose of 18 mSv.[3] This is more than the average radiation dose during coronary angiography, which is in the order of 10 mSv. ^{201}Tl is excreted mainly by the kidney and this is the critical organ. The whole-body biological half-life is around 10 days.

Myocardial distribution

Distribution within the myocardium is proportional to blood flow over a wide range of values although at high rates of flow, extraction becomes rate limiting. Once within the heart the half-life of elimination is approximately 7 h. The slow washout may be explained either by binding within the cell or by the adverse electropotential gradient.

Patient preparation and imaging protocol

Thallium is given at peak stress, which is continued for 2 min to maintain stable conditions over the period of extraction of tracer by the myocardium. Stress imaging should begin within 5 min of injection and should be completed within 30 min to minimise the effects of redistribution. During this period the distribution of thallium within the myocardium remains relatively fixed, and despite the cessation of exercise the images reflect myocardial perfusion at peak stress. Redistribution images are taken 3-4 h after the stress images. Infusion of glucose and insulin in animals increases the clearance of thallium from the myocardium, and food ingested after stress imaging in humans has been shown to reduce redistribution.[4] Stress images should therefore be acquired after light meals only, unless the patient is diabetic, and fasting is recommended between stress and redistribution imaging. By contrast, ribose infusion after stress may hasten redistribution, and the clinical value of this is under investigation.[5,6] This effect appears to be the result of enhanced clearance of thallium from normal myocardium.[7]

Redistribution

There is slow equilibration between intracellular and intravascular thallium, so that the myocardial pattern of distribution changes. With this redistribution, the images obtained several hours after injection are similar to those that would have been obtained had the thallium been injected at rest. The mechanism of redistribution probably results partly from differential washout, as washout is proportional to the rate of coronary flow, and also from tracer uptake into areas of low uptake from the persistent thallium blood activity.

A normal region shows high uptake after stress but rapid washout. In areas supplied by functionally significant stenoses, evidence of reversible ischaemia is seen as a stress defect which improves in the redistribution images. An infarcted area appears as a fixed defect, which is a stress defect that fails to improve on redistribution imaging. Mixed patterns may also be seen: partial infarction shows as a fixed defect with moderate intensity uptake, and partial infarction with reversible ischaemia shows as a stress defect with partial but not complete reversibility.

Under normal circumstances, uptake in the redistribution image reflects the amount of muscle present, and the uptake in the stress image reflects the amount of muscle present modulated by stress perfusion. Recently, however, very slow redistribution in ischaemic but non-infarcted myocardium has been shown to occur when the artery supplying the territory is severely stenosed or occluded, and resting perfusion may be reduced. Thallium reinjection after the stress/redistribution study, or an injection at rest on a separate day with early and delayed imaging, may then be necessary to accurately delineate the total myocardial mass present. This prevents the overdiagnosis of infarction, and underestimation of residual muscle mass in areas of partial infarction.

Lung uptake

In normal volunteers 5%-15% of the injected dose is extracted by the lungs before reaching the systemic circulation. In patients with left ventricular failure and a high pulmonary capillary wedge pressure, the amount extracted by the lungs is greater and there may even be significant lung uptake at rest. When this occurs, the heart to lung counts ratio is reduced, and this has been shown to be prognostically important.

Thallium has been used as a myocardial perfusion tracer for almost 20 years and the experience collected over this time is considerable. Despite the limitations of ^{201}Tl, it is the standard against which other tracers must be judged. To overcome the limitations of ^{201}Tl, agents labelled with ^{99m}Tc have been developed, including ^{99m}Tc-MIBI and ^{99m}Tc-tetrofosmin.

^{99m}Tc-MIBI

Basic properties

^{99m}Tc-MIBI is produced by Du Pont with the trade name Cardiolite. ^{99m}Tc-MIBI consists of six methoxyisobutyl-isonitrile molecules complexing an atom of ^{99m}Tc. It is lipophilic and after injection it distributes in the myocardium in proportion to blood flow. ^{99m}Tc-MIBI diffuses out of the capillary into cardiac myocytes and is associated with mitochondria within the cell.[8] Cardiac uptake of ^{99m}Tc-MIBI is therefore dependent on normal mitochondrial function. Uptake is depressed and washout increased when there is cellular hypoxia secondary to severe myocardial ischaemia. Its clearance from blood is rapid, with a half-life of 2 min, but the first-pass extraction (40%–60%) is lower than thallium.[9] Retention of MIBI in the myocardium is better however, and after approximately 20 min the percentage of the injected dose in the myocardium is similar for both tracers.[10]

Myocardial distribution

Unlike ^{201}Tl, ^{99m}Tc-MIBI only redistributes by 10%-15% from its pattern of initial uptake, which is not usually clinically significant. In a dog study the ratio of ^{99m}Tc-MIBI activity in normal and ischaemic areas did not change over the 4 h following injection. The lack of redistribution allows imaging studies to be performed up to several hours after injection if necessary, which can be very useful if the stress room is a long distance from the camera, or if imaging of perfusion in highly dynamic situations such as thrombolysis is required.

Patient preparation and imaging protocol

The absence of redistribution means that two separate injections are required to compare stress and resting perfusion. The 6-h half-life of ^{99m}Tc means that ideally the two studies should be performed on separate days if residual activity from the first injection is not to confuse the images acquired after the second

9

injection. Alternatively, the two studies may be performed on the same day if a three to five times larger dose is given on the second occasion to swamp activity from the first injection.

In the 2-day protocol, the stress study is normally performed first and if this is normal a rest study may not be required. In the 1-day protocol the rest study is normally performed before the stress study. The consensus view is that the 2-day protocol is preferable, even though the 1-day protocol provides quicker results.

A disadvantage of ^{99m}Tc-MIBI is the high hepatobiliary uptake that occurs in the first hour after injection, which may interfere with interpretation of cardiac activity in the inferior wall. Milk or chocolate has been given 15 min after injection of ^{99m}Tc-MIBI to stimulate gallbladder contraction and liver clearance, but the value of this has been questioned.[11] Best contrast between myocardial and liver uptake is obtained in images acquired approximately 1 h after injection. The other main disadvantages of ^{99m}Tc-MIBI are cost, that preparation involves boiling, and that the reconstituted product has a shelf-life of only 6 h.

Dosimetry

The maximum UK dose recommended by ARSAC is 300 MBq for planar imaging and 400 MBq for tomography for the 2-day protocol. For the 1-day protocol, total doses of 800 MBq and 1000 MBq respectively are permitted. For tomography the typical dose split used would be 250 MBq/750 MBq for the two injections. The injection of 1000 MBq ^{99m}Tc-MIBI is associated with an effective dose equivalent of approximately 8 mSv. Highest concentrations of activity are found in the liver, gallbladder and heart. Activity accumulating in the liver and gallbladder is excreted into the bowel, which receives the highest radiation dose and is therefore the critical organ.

^{99M}Tc-TETROFOSMIN

Basic properties

The trade name for ^{99m}Tc-tetrofosmin is Myoview (produced by Amersham International), and this has been licensed for clinical use in the UK since 1994. ^{99m}Tc-tetrofosmin is lipophilic and is rapidly cleared from the blood after intravenous injection, with less than 5% residual activity by 10 min.[12] Uptake in the myocardium is rapid, reaching a maximum of 1.2% of the injected dose within 5 min. ^{99m}Tc-tetrofosmin shows little if any redistribution over 4 h. Liver uptake is not as prominent as with ^{99m}Tc-MIBI.[13] The mechanism of myocardial uptake is again related to diffusion along an electropotential gradient as demonstrated *in vitro* by uptake studies using isolated myocytes and isolated mitochondria.[14,15] It is regionally distributed within the myocardium in proportion to blood flow at the time of injection.[16]

Imaging protocol

Separate injections are required for rest and stress imaging. Imaging should begin no earlier than 15 min after injection with optimum images beung obtained from approximately 30-45 min. As there is little or no redistribution of ^{99m}Tc–tetrofosmin, images may be acquired up to 4 h after injection. Because of the more rapid clearance a 1-day protocol has been found to be satisfactory.[13] This allows for improved flexibility in the busy clinic. In practice local factors and patient logistics will likely determine the choice between 1-day or 2-day methods. Comparisons of imaging with thallium in coronary artery disease demonstrate good clinical agreement.[17,18] The radiopharmacy preparation is quite straight forward with labelling in the kiy vial at room temperature.

Dosimetry

For stress imaging 250 MBq is given at peak exercise. Rest imaging can be performed 4 h later and a dose of 750 MBq is injected. ARSAC requires that the activity administered should be restricted to 1000 MBq for SPET imging using a 1-day protocol. The effective dose equivalent resulting from the 1-day protocol with 1000 MBq is approximately 8 mSv, and that resulting from the 2-day protocol, 6 mSv. No boiling is required in the preparation of this agent. Table 1. compares some characteristics of the three main perfusion agents.

Advantages of ^{99m}Tc Tetrofosmin and ^{99m}Tc-MIBI over ^{201}TL

Myocardial images have higher spatial resolution and higher count densities because of the higher energy photon produced by ^{99m}Tc (140 keV) and its short 6-h half-life, which allows larger doses to be given with a lower radiation burden.

The higher count density allows gated perfusion tomograms, thereby permitting assessment of regional wall motion and wall thickening. Alternatively, ^{99m}Tc-agents may be administered as a bolus and a first-pass assessment of right and left ventricular function performed. Attenuation secondary to the interposition of other tissues such as breasts is also less. Finally, because ^{99m}Tc is generator produced, it is cheap and readily available. In clinical practice, ^{99m}Tc-agents give at least the same sensitivity and specificity for the detection of coronary artery disease as thallium.

Advantages of the lack of redistribution

The lack of redistribution of ^{99m}Tc-agents means that patients can be imaged at geographically distant locations from the site of exercise testing without loss of data. Further, imaging can be repeated without loss of sensitivity in the event of patient motion. Imaging can also be delayed for some time after injection, which is particularly useful in patients with acute myocardial infarction. ^{99m}Tc-agents may be injected before thrombolysis but imaged much later when the patient is clinically stable. The images taken at this time delineate the extent of myocardium at risk whilst a later injection allows the amount of myocardium salvaged by thrombolysis to be estimated.

^{99M}Tc-TEBOROXIME
Basic properties

The trade name for ^{99m}Tc-teboroxime is Cardiotec; it is manufactured by Squibb, but is only licensed for use in the USA. As yet it is still to gain widespread acceptance for routine application. Like ^{99m}Tc–tetrofosmin and ^{99m}Tc-MIBI, this agent is highly lipophilic and after injection is regionally distributed in the myocardium in proportion to blood flow.

	Thallium-201	^{99m}Tc-MIBI	^{99m}Tc-Tetrofosmin
Class	Element	Isonitrile	Diphosphine
Charge	Cation	Cation	Cation
Initial myocardial uptake (%)	4	1.5	1.2
Uptake relation to flow increase	Good	Adequate	Adequate
Typical imaging time post-injection (min)	5	60	20
Typical number of injections	1	2	2
Redistribution	Yes	Minimal	No
First pass	No	Yes	Yes
Gated ventricular function	Possibly	Yes	Yes
Excretion	Kidney	Gut	Gut and kidney
Activity (MBq)	80	1000 (1 day) 800 (2 day)	1000 (1 day) 800 (2 day)
Dosimetry (mSv)	18	8 (1 day) 6 (2 day)	8 (1 day) 6 (2 day)

Table 1 *Characteristics of the various perfusion agents*

Myocardial uptake is evident by 1 min after injection and occurs by diffusion. Following intravenous injection approximately 90% of the dose is cleared from the blood after the first circulation. The proportion of the injected dose taken up by the myocardium is relatively high, being more than 3% at 1 min. Myocardial washout begins within a few minutes of intravenous injection. Differential washout provides the equivalent of some redistribution.[19,20]

Imaging protocol

Separate injections of teboroxime are required for stress and rest imaging and can be given 1-2 h apart. Imaging can be started 2-3 min after injection but must be completed very rapidly and preferably within 10 min of injection if good-quality images with a high cardiac count density are to be produced. In this time span planar imaging is possible but tomography is difficult unless a multiheaded gamma camera is used. Hepatic activity is prominent by 5-10 min and can interfere with visualisation of the inferior wall.

References

1. Weich HF, Strauss HW, Pitt B. The extraction of thallium-201 by the myocardium. *Circulation* 1977; **56**: 188-91

2. Leppo JA. Myocardial uptake of thallium and rubidium during alterations in perfusion and oxygenation in isolated rabbit hearts. *J Nucl Med* 1987; **28**: 875-85.

3. Johansson L, Mattsson S, Nosslin B, Leide-Svegborn S. Effective dose from radiopharmaceuticals. *Eur J Nucl Med* 1992; **19**: 933-8.

4. Wilson RA, Sullivan PJ, Okada RD, et al. The effect of eating on thallium myocardial imaging. *Chest* 1986; **89**: 195-8.

5. Perlmutter NS, Wilson RA, Angello DA, Palac RT, Lin J, Brown BG. Ribose facilitates thallium-201 redistribution in patients with coronary artery disease. *J Nucl Med* 1991; **32**: 193-200.

6. Hegewald MG, Palac RT, Angello DA, Perlmutter NS, Wilson RA. Ribose infusion accelerates thallium redistribution with early imaging compared with late 24 hour imaging without ribose. *J Am Coll Cardiol* 1991; **18**: 1671-81.

7. Angello DA, Wilson RA, Gee D. The effect of ribose on postischemic thallium-201 kinetics. *J Nucl Med* 1988; **29**: 1943-50.

8. Carvalho PA, Chiu ML, Kronauge JF, et al. Subcellular distribution and analysis of technetium-99m MIBI in isolated perfused rat hearts. *J Nucl Med* 1992; **33**: 1516-22.

9. Leppo JA, Johnson LL. A review of cardiac imaging with sestamibi and teboroxime. *J Nucl Med* 1991; **32**: 2012-22.

10. Melon PG, Beanlands RS, DeGrado TR, Nguyen N, Petry NA, Schwaiger M. Comparison of technetium-99m sestamibi and thallium-201 retention characteristics in canine myocardium. *J Am Coll Cardiol* 1992; **20**: 1277-83.

11. Hurwitz GA, Clark EM, Slomka PG, Siddiq SK. Investigation of measures to reduce interfering abdominal activity on rest myocardial images with Tc-99m sestamibi. *Clin Nucl Med* 1993; **9**: 735-41.

12. Higley B, Smith FW, Smith T, et al. Technetium-99m-1,2-bis (2-ethoxyethyl) phosphino]ethane: human biodistribution, dosimetry and safety of a new myocardial perfusion imaging agent. *J Nucl Med* 1994; **34**: 30-8.

13. Jain D, Wackers FJ, Mattera J, McMahon M, Sinusas AJ, Zaret BL. Biokinetics of technetium-99m-tetrofosmin: Myocardial perfusion imaging agent: implications for a one-day imaging protocol. *J Nucl Med* 1993; **34**: 1254-9.

14. Platts EA, North TL, Pickett RD, Kelly JD. Mechanism of uptake of Tc-tetrofosmin. I. Uptake into isolated adult rat myocytes and subcellular localisation. *J Nuc Cardiol* 1995 in press.

15. Younès A, Songadele JA, Maublant J, Platts EA, Pickett RD, Veyre A. Mechanism of uptake of Tc-tetrofosmin. II. Uptake into isolated adult rat heart mitochondria. *J Nuc Cardiol* 1995, in press.

16. Sinusas AJ, Shi QX, Saltzberg MT, et al. Technetium-99m-tetrofosmin to assess myocardial blood flow: experimental validation in an intact canine model of ischemia. *J Nucl Med* 1994; **35**: 664-71.

17. Sridhara BS, Braat S, Rigo P, et al. Comparison of myocardial perfusion imaging with technetium-99m-tetrofosmin versus thallium-201 in coronary artery disease. *Am J Cardiol* 1993; **72**: 1015-9.

18. Zaret BL, Rigo P, Wackers FJT, Hendel RC, Braat SH, Iskandrian AS, Sridhara BS, Jain D, Itti R, Serafini AN, Goris ML, Lahiri A. Myocardial perfusion imaging with ^{99m}Tc tetrofosmin. Comparison to ^{201}Tl imaging and coronary angiography in a phase III multicentre trial. *Circulation* 1995; **91**: 313-319.

19. Chua T, Kiat H, Germano G, et al. Technetium-99m teboroxime regional myocardial washout in subjects with and without coronary artery disease. *Am J Cardiol* 1993; 9: 728-34.

20. Chiao PC, Ficaro EP, Dayanikli F, Rogers WL, Schwaiger M. Compartmental analysis of Tc-99m-teboroxime kinetics with fast dynamic SPECT at rest and stress. *J Nucl Med* 1994; 35: 1265-73.

Imaging Techniques

THE GAMMA CAMERA

Nuclear medicine images of the heart are almost invariably acquired with a gamma camera.[1] The camera detects the scintillations (flashes of light) produced when gamma rays interact with a sodium iodide crystal at the front of the camera. The scintillations are detected by photomultiplier tubes, and whilst the areas of crystal seen by the tubes overlap, the location of each scintillation can be computed from the relative responses in each tube. The energy of each scintillation is also measured from the response of the tubes, and the electrical signal to the imaging computer consists of the location and photon energy. In front of the crystal is a collimator which is made of lead with multiple elongated holes. The holes allow only gamma rays that are travelling perpendicularly to the crystal face to enter. The gamma photons absorbed by the crystal therefore form an image of the distribution of radionuclide in front of the camera. The camera rotates around the patient to perform emission tomography.

EMISSION TOMOGRAPHY

Emission tomography using radionuclides was first described in 1963,[2] but only in the last 10 years has the performance of the imaging hardware and reconstruction software led to its widespread use in nuclear medicine.[3,4] In nuclear cardiology, tomography has been widely adopted for myocardial perfusion imaging and also sometimes for acute infarct imaging, but gated blood pool emission tomography has lagged behind, because of the computing requirements.[5,6]

Whilst planar imaging has been the normal method of image acquisition in general nuclear medicine, it suffers from the disadvantage that it is difficult to separate the activity from overlapping structures. Multiple projections can be helpful, and it is usual to acquire anterior, left anterior oblique and left lateral images. The technique also suffers from poor clinical acceptability, however, because the image projections fail to resemble the tomographic image planes of other cardiological investigations, most importantly echocardiography. One of the most important but seldom appreciated aspects of tomography is that it enables cardiologists to really develop an interest in the images and compare their experience with the report in the clinical setting. The improved involvement leads to greater interest and familiarity, which enables the clinician to develop clinical management schemes which involve, rather than ignore, nuclear cardiology. A further small but important issue is the usual representation of the tomographic images in colour rather than black and white. This seemingly trivial step again considerably aids acceptability, not only by improving the presentation, but also by making the images easier to interpret (Table 1).

- Improved resolution

- Differentiation of overlapping myocardial regions

- Depiction in planes familiar to cardiologists

- Comparability with other cardiological imaging techniques such as echocardiography

- Colour images improve interpretation and presentation

- Improved sensitivity and specificity of diagnosis

- Depiction of images in same orientation irrespective of cardiac position

- Improved clinical acceptance and development of further interest

Table 1 *Advantages of tomography over planar perfusion imaging*

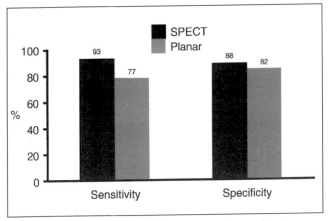

Fig. 1. *Sensitivity and specificity results in five studies comparing planar and tomographic imaging, suggesting superiority of tomography for diagnosis of coronary artery disease. (Data from J Nucl Med 1982; 23: 204, Circulation 1982; 66: 370, Am J Cardiol 1982; 50: 1236, J Nucl Med 1983; 24: 761, Eur J Nucl Med 1984; 9: 99)*

One other extremely important point in considering the comparison between planar and tomographic imaging is the sensitivity of the scan for detecting significant coronary artery disease. This issue is now resolved in favour of tomographic imaging. There have been two approaches to the demonstration of superiority of tomography. The first is the direct comparison of sensitivity and specificity of the two techniques, which favours tomography for both measures; this is shown in Fig. 1. The second and more rigorous approach is to use receiver operating characteristic analysis. Briefly, this technique plots sensitivity against the false-positive fraction to make the comparison between techniques using an arbitrary series of diagnostic thresholds to form multiple points on the curve. Comparisons between the techniques can then be made using the area under each curve. The results of this analysis in the comparison of planar imaging and tomography clearly demonstrate improved diagnosis of coronary artery disease with tomography (Fig. 2).[7]

The technique of tomography relies on the acquisition of a number of equally spaced planar views (typically 32) as the

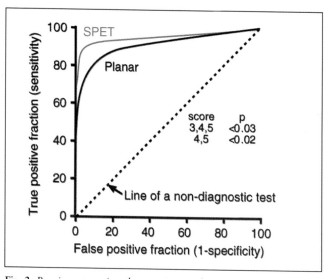

Fig. 2. *Receiver operating characteristic analysis of planar and tomographic myocardial perfusion imaging with thallium.*
The sensitivity is plotted on the vertical scale with the false-positive fraction (1-specificity) on the horizontal scale. The ideal investigation yields a curve, which over the range of possible decision thresholds passes directly up the vertical scale to 100% sensitivity, before turning horizontally to the top right corner, which represents 100% specificity. No real investigation ever achieves this ideal, and comparison between techniques can be made by comparing the area under each curve. The curve for tomography is seen to lie above the planar curve, a result which was statistically significant, showing that tomography is superior to planar imaging for diagnosis of coronary artery disease. (Reproduced with permission[7])

camera rotates around the patient. These are then reconstructed into tomograms using backprojection algorithms which estimate the original three-dimensional distribution of activity that would have resulted in the planar views actually obtained. Tomography also has technical advantages over planar imaging which include improved image contrast because of the elimination of overlying structures, and the potential for quantification of the tracer uptake.

Quality control of the system is vital for the acquisition of good-quality emission tomograms, and here the role of the physicist is vital. Daily uniformity checks and regular centre of rotation acquisition are important, and other technical aspects must also be constantly attended to. The penalty for inattention to the technical quality is imaging artefacts causing false-positive results, or uninterpretable images. From the acquisition standpoint, it is always important to ensure good patient comfort before starting the scan to prevent movement, and great care should be taken to ensure that the camera orbit is as close to the patient as possible. The main secret of good-quality tomography is attention to important details, as are listed in Table 2.

PATIENT PREPARATION

The perfusion tracer is injected at peak stress, using an intravenous cannula in the largest available arm vein. If the injection is mistakenly given outside the vein no harm usually results, although there is the theoretical risk of localised radiation necrosis. A more important problem with an injection which is partly extravascular is that the quality of the images will suffer. After the thallium injection, the syringe should be flushed with 10-20 ml of saline from a second syringe connected via a three-way tap, to ensure that the full dose of thallium is administered.

For imaging, the patient lies supine on the couch with the left arm above the head. This position is uncomfortable, particularly for elderly patients with cervical spine or shoulder problems, but the majority of patients will tolerate the position for 15-20 min. A pillow placed under the knees gives some comfort and helps the patient to keep still. This is important because motion artefacts may not be easily identified after the acquisition. The arm needs to be raised above the head so that it does not cause attenuation in the lateral projections and so that the camera can be as close as possible to the chest wall. For cameras which rotate in a circular orbit the positions which limit the proximity of the camera are usually the right shoulder and the left arm. For cameras which rotate in non-circular orbits, better approximation of the camera to the chest wall can be achieved at all parts of the orbit.

21

TECHNICAL ASPECTS

- Regular quality control checks of camera are essential and should include weekly centre of rotation measurements and uniformity correction acquisitions of 3×10^7 counts.

- The camera rotation must be as close to the chest wall as possible.

- Patient comfort is vital to prevent movement artefact.

CLINICAL ASPECTS

- The thallium must be injected at peak stress. It is becoming increasingly common for pharmacological stress to supplant exercise for this purpose because of the high incidence of poor exercise for physical or psychological reasons. Pharmacological stress is reliable and its control is independent of the patient.

- The clinical assessment during stress is useful and is an essential part of the report. Clinical assessment of the patient's history during the visit is often illuminating in completing the clinical picture of the referral, which is often accompanied by scarce detail.

- There must be close liaison between the requesting clinician, the doctor performing the scan, and the reporter. Ideally, the three should be the same. Failing this, the clinical question must be clearly defined and the consequences of the findings must be clearly understood by the reporting doctor. Failure to appreciate this point will lead to inappropriate reports and management decisions, and confidence in the service will be eroded.

Table 2 *Some guidelines for reliable tomographic perfusion imaging*

Artefacts will be caused by any attenuating structure which comes between the heart and the camera. Metallic objects in pockets and metal buttons must be avoided but it is sometimes difficult to avoid the artefact from an implanted pacemaker. In ladies with large breasts, the site of artefact in the tomograms will depend upon where the breast attenuates the planar images. It is recommended that the breasts are strapped against the chest so that the attenuation is as uniform as possible. Prone imaging is another possibility although the images tend to be of poorer quality. The left hemi-diaphragm will also cause attenuation if it is elevated by, for instance, a large meal. For this reason, light nourishment only before imaging is recommended.

DATA ACQUISITION

The ideal tomographic acquisition spans 360° with as many steps as possible but, in practice, this leads to prolonged imaging times. In fact, rotation of the camera over only 180° will yield sufficient data, and this is the usual clinical practice. The heart is well suited to this because it lies in the left anterior thorax and the posterior images are severely degraded by attenuation. This has been established for thallium emission tomography[8] although there is some dispute.[9,10,11] Tables 3 and 4 summarise the acquisition parameters which are typically used for ^{201}Tl and ^{99m}Tc perfusion imaging respectively.

The stress images are acquired as soon as possible after the end of exercise and should be completed within 30 min. Redistribution images are usually acquired 4 h after injection but redistribution imaging is sometimes performed earlier without loss of diagnostic accuracy. This avoids excessive loss of thallium from the heart at the time of imaging. Imaging at 24 h is sometimes performed when the question of underestimation of myocardial mass in the redistribution images is clinically important. The image quality with these very late images is poor however, and increasingly a second thallium injection on a separate day or immediately after the redistribution images is being performed. This is at the expense of an increased radiation burden to the patient.

In suitable clinical circumstances, normal stress images may avoid the need for redistribution imaging. There is no circumstance in which a study could be considered abnormal if the stress images are unequivocally normal.

Number of heads on camera	2
Number of projections	64
Time per projection	20 s stress, 25 s redistribution
Acquisition time	11 min stress, 14 min redistribution
Type of orbit	Non-circular or body contoured if available
Arc of rotation	180°
Collimator	High-resolution, parallel-hole
Photopeaks	80, 167 keV
Energy window, offset	20%, 0
Image size	40 cm unzoomed, 64 x 64 pixels

Table 3 *Ideal imaging parameters for ^{201}Tl myocardial perfusion imaging*

Number of heads on camera	2
Number of projections	64
Time per projection	20 s stress and rest
Acquisition time	11 min
Type of orbit	Non-circular or body contoured
Arc of rotation	180°
Collimator	High-resolution, parallel-hole
Photopeaks	140 keV
Energy window	20%
Image size	40 cm unzoomed, 64 x 64 pixels

Table 4 *Ideal acquisition parameters for perfusion imaging with ^{99m}Tc-labelled agents*

DATA PROCESSING

The set of planar images is reconstructed into a stack of transaxial tomograms by filtered backprojection. This projects a modified form of each of the planar images into three-dimensional space, such that there is reinforcement at the true position of a source of activity but no reinforcement at other positions. The final result is a reconstructed distribution of activity which is consistent with all the projection images that were acquired, and with modern techniques the uncertainty of the reconstructed activity distribution is minimised.

ATTENUATION CORRECTION

Gamma photons are attenuated in passing through the body, and the more superficial structures therefore exhibit higher counts in the images. This causes problems in several circumstances, and in addition prevents the quantification of the images in terms of absolute myocardial blood flow. There are a number of methods of estimating attenuation and correcting activity from deeper structures, but none is clinically robust or suitable for a 180° acquisition. However, recent technical advances suggest that the situation may now improve, because several manufacturers have now developed simultaneous emission and transmission tomography. An external line source is commonly used to generate a comparable set of transmission images to the emission images. The two data sets together can be used for attenuation correction. Early results have shown that inferior wall activity, which is commonly low in normal males, increases substantially to be equivalent to the far less attenuated anterior wall.

OBLIQUE IMAGE REORIENTATION

The series of transaxial slices is a three-dimensional data set and the data are simply reorientated into oblique slices. For the heart, the most useful oblique planes are the vertical and horizontal long-axis (VLA and HLA) and the short-axis planes (SA). These planes pass perpendicularly through the major left ventricular walls and they are familiar to cardiologists from other imaging techniques. This enhances interpretation and acceptance by cardiologists without nuclear medicine training and allows a direct comparison of perfusion with functional or anatomical measures such as wall motion.[12] In order to define the angles of the planes, a central transaxial slice is displayed on the computer screen and the long axis is drawn on this image. Perpendicular to the transaxial plane and including the long axis as drawn, the vertical long-axis slices are reconstructed. From the central vertical long-axis slice, the caudal inclination of the true long axis can be seen and the horizontal long-axis and short-axis slices can be generated, both perpendicular to the vertical long-axis slices.

IMAGING PROTOCOLS FOR THALLIUM PERFUSION IMAGING

There is little controversy regarding the stress protocol for ^{201}Tl imaging, with immediate post-stress imaging being followed usually 3-4 h later by redistribution imaging. No separate resting injection is required in the majority of these studies. The issue of accurate estimation of residual myocardial mass present in an area of infarction, or in an area with very poor blood supply, will be covered in the chapter on myocardial hibernation. Suffice to say at this point that redistribution may be very slow if thallium supply to an area of myocardium is severely impaired, and standard redistribution imaging may underestimate the amount of myocardial tissue present, or reversible ischaemia in this area. Further thallium injections at rest are then required.

STRESS PROTOCOLS FOR ^{99M}Tc PERFUSION AGENTS

The relatively recent development of ^{99m}Tc-labelled perfusion tracers for the heart has greatly increased interest in comparative imaging protocols. The technetium agents have some advantages over thallium as listed in Table 5, and their disadvantages are shown in Table 6.

- Higher energy photon emission reduces attenuation problems, which is particularly useful in the obese patient or women with large breasts.

- The link between stress and immediate imaging is broken, such that injection can take place in sites remote from the camera such as the exercise stress department, the emergency room or the coronary care unit with later imaging.

- The injected bolus can be followed with first- pass imaging to investigate ventricular function.

- The high count rates allow gated tomography which enables wall motion and wall thickening to be investigated.

- There is a significantly lower radiation burden to the patient.

- The kit for reconstitution and the ^{99m}Tc are readily available.

- Improved image quality

- Improved certainty of diagnosis, and lower interobserver variability for interpretation

Table 5 *Advantages of ^{99m}Tc agents over ^{201}Tl for perfusion imaging*

Unlike stress/redistribution ^{201}Tl perfusion imaging, which requires just a single injection, when the ^{99m}Tc agents are used a double-injection technique is required. The order of the injections and whether to perform a 1- or 2-day protocol has been the subject of much discussion.[13] The practice in various centres is naturally biased according to local habits, referral patterns and experience, and there is no single protocol to suit all situations. There is general agreement on several points, however, some of which are conflicting (Table 7): (a) the 2-day protocol is the most reliable, because residual activity from the first injection is insignificant by the next day; (b) the 2-day protocol has the advantage of two injections of similar and reasonable activity (400 MBq) which yield good-quality

27

- Unless there is reasonable patient throughput, the reconstitution of a vial for less than several patients in a day is expensive.

- The ideal imaging protocol is over 2 days with the stress injection on day 1, but this is unsuitable for some patients, particularly if travelling long distances. It may also be less than ideal for inpatients awaiting management decisions.

- A clinical issue remains unresolved as to whether the technetium agents may underestimate myocardial mass in areas where the resting blood supply is reduced, because ^{99m}Tc tracer delivery is low. In this regard, ^{201}Tl has a *theoretical* advantage because in time it redistributes into such areas, and late images reflect muscle mass relatively independent of resting perfusion. Further studies are required to clarify the situation.

- Hepatobiliary activity may sometimes cause problems in the interpretation of the inferior wall.

Table 6 *Disadvantages of ^{99m}Tc agents for perfusion imaging*

images for both studies, and is associated with a lower radiation burden than the 1-day protocol; (c) if feasible, the performance of the stress imaging first, allows physician interaction to prevent the administration of an unnecessary rest injection when the stress images are unequivocally normal;[14] and (d), when patients travel long distances for the study, the 2-day protocol is not ideal, and the 1-day protocol is usually necessary. In the UK in 1993, approximately 85% of studies with the ^{99m}Tc agents were performed with a 2-day protocol,[15] which implies that most nuclear cardiology practitioners have placed the imaging requirements ahead of possible patient inconvenience.

There are studies in the literature which directly compare the protocols and these throw light on the problems that the 1–day protocol may cause. Comparison of a rest-stress with a stress-rest 1-day technique showed that the rest-stress protocol had advantages in demonstrating ischaemia in segments which

- The 2-day protocol gives the best results and is the most sound scientifically.

- The 1-day protocol is more convenient for many patients, particularly if travelling long distances.

- In general, a rest-stress order for the 1-day protocol is preferred, because the clearer depiction of rest perfusion identifies reversible ischaemia more reliably, it yields better contrast in the counts between the rest and stress images, stress first-pass imaging and wall motion can be performed with the higher dose second injection, and overall the dosimetry is slightly lower.

- For the 1-day protocol, in patients with known abnormalities of resting perfusion, such as previous myocardial infarction, the rest injection should be given first.

- For the 1-day protocol, if there is a low pre-test likelihood of coronary artery disease, the first injection should be with stress such that the resting injection might be avoided.

- For the 2-day protocol the first injection should routinely be with stress, in case the resting study can be avoided.

- The use of a standard protocol for the majority of patients attending for perfusion imaging aids considerably in the streamlining of patient throughput.

Table 7 *Some factors to be considered for imaging protocols with the ^{99m}Tc agents*

were thought to be fixed by the stress-rest protocol.[16] This arises because when the rest injection is given first, a clear delineation of the size and severity of any resting defect is shown, but when the stress injection is given first, which creates a significant stress defect, the subsequent rest injection may not be able to fill this in. This problem arose in 7.4% of segments studied and certainly favours the initial use of resting rather than stress injection. There are other advantages to the

rest-stress approach: (a) since the cardiac uptake of
⁹⁹ᵐTc agents is higher at stress than rest, there is a greater ratio
of myocardial counts between the first and second injections
when the first, lower dose is given at rest, and this improves
contrast and helps to limit interference in interpretation from
residual activity from the first injection; (b) because the
dosimetry is lower for the stress injection, the radiation
burden to the patient is slightly lower if the larger second
injection is during stress; (c) when the second, larger injection
is given during stress, a first-pass stress radionuclide
angiogram can be acquired, but if stress is performed with the
first, lower dose injection, there are insufficient counts for
good results; and (d), the results of this protocol have been
shown to be amenable to a quantitative analysis.[17]

Unfortunately, despite the advantages of using a resting
injection first, some problems still persist, and once again
these are due to persistent activity in areas of normal
perfusion at rest which become only mildly ischaemic with
stress. The residual activity from the normal resting injection
in the area of abnormal stress perfusion can mask the
detection of the stress defect. This problem occurred in
approximately 4% of segments in one study.[18]

OTHER CARDIAC IMAGING TECHNIQUES WITH THE ⁹⁹ᴹTc PERFUSION AGENTS

The high injected dose allows first-pass imaging of ventricular
function and it has been suggested that significant diagnostic
information can be gained from the combined perfusion/
function data. The method is technically reasonably
straightforward,[19] and compares well with other first-pass
techniques.[20] Gating of the tomographic images also allows wall
motion and thickening to be assessed,[21,22] and this may add to
the diagnostic information from perfusion alone.[23] Gating has
also proved useful in distinguishing areas of attenuation from
partial infarction by the demonstration of completely normal
wall motion in the former case. The improved resolution of

^{99m}Tc images has also allowed the investigation of right ventricular regional perfusion with reversible defects commonly shown in right coronary artery disease.[24]

References

1. Anger H. Scintillation camera. *The Review of Scientific Instruments* 1958; **29**: 27-33.

2. Kuhl DE, Edwards RQ. Image separation radioisotope scanning. *Radiology* 1963; **80**: 653-61.

3. Ell PJ, Holman BL. Computed emission tomography. Oxford: *Oxford Med Pub*, 1982.

4. Ell PJ, Jarritt PH. Gamma camera emission tomography; quality control and clinical applications. London: Chapman and Hall, 1984.

5. Tamaki N, Mukai T, Ishii Y, et al. Multiaxial tomography of heart chambers by gated blood-pool emission computed tomography using a rotating gamma camera. *Radiology* 1983; **147**: 547-54.

6. Underwood SR, Walton S, Ell PJ, Jarritt PH, Emanuel RW, Swanton RH. Gated blood-pool emission tomography: a new technique for the investigation of cardiac structure and function. *Eur J Nucl Med* 1985; **10**: 332-7.

7. Fintel DJ, Links, Brinker JA, Frank TL, Parker M, Becker LC. Improved diagnostic performance of exercise thallium-201 single photon emission computed tomography over planar imaging in the diagnosis of coronary artery disease: a receiver operating characteristic analysis. *J Am Coll Cardiol* 1989; **13**: 600-12.

8. Hoffman EJ. 180° compared with 360° sampling in SPECT. *J Nucl Med* 1982; **23**: 745-7.

9. Coleman RE, Jaszczak RJ, Cobb FR. Comparison of 180 deg and 360 deg data collection in thallium-201 imaging using single photon emission computed tomography (SPECT). *J Nucl Med* 1982; **23**: 655-60.

10. Go RT, McIntyre WJ, Houser TS, et al. Clinical evaluation of 360° and 180° data sampling techniques for transaxial SPECT thallium-201 myocardial perfusion imaging. *J Nucl Med* 1985; **26**: 695-706.

11. Knesaurek K. Image distortion in 180° SPECT studies. *J Nucl Med* 1986; **27**: 1792.

12. Pennell DJ, Underwood SR, Ell PJ, Swanton RH, Walker JM, Longmore DB. Dipyridamole magnetic resonance imaging: a comparison with thallium-201 emission tomography. *Br Heart J* 1990; **64**: 362-9.

13. Berman DS, Kiat HS, Vantrain KF, Germano G, Maddahi J, Friedman JD. Myocardial perfusion imaging with technetium-99m-sestamibi–comparative analysis of available imaging protocols. *J Nucl Med* 1994; **35**: 681-8.

14. Worsley DF, Fung AY, Coupland DB, Rexworthy CG, Sexsmith GP, Lentle BC. Comparison of stress only vs stress/rest with technetium-99m methoxyisobutylisonitrile myocardial perfusion imaging. *Eur J Nucl Med* 1992; **19**: 441-4.

15. Pennell DJ, Caplin J, Prvulovich E. British Nuclear Cardiology Group: survey of UK nuclear cardiology practice 1993 (abstract). *Br Heart J* 1995; in press.

16. Taillefer R, Gagnon A, Laflamme L, Gregoire J, Leveille J, Phaneuf D. Same day injections of Tc-99m methoxy isobutyl isonitrile (hexamibi) for myocardial tomographic imaging: comparison between rest-stress and stress-rest injection sequences. *Eur J Nucl Med* 1989; **15**: 113-7.

17. Vantrain KF, Garcia EV, Maddahi J, et al. Multicenter trial validation for quantitative analysis of same-day rest-stress technetium-99m-sestamibi myocardial tomograms. *J Nucl Med* 1994; **4**: 609-18.

18. Heo J, Kegel J, Iskandrian AS, Cave VB, Iskandrian BB. Comparison of same day protocols using technetium-99m-sestamibi myocardial imaging. *J Nucl Med* 1992; **33**: 186–91.

19. Iskandrian AS, Heo J, Kong B, Lyons E, Marsch S. Use of technetium-99m isonitrile (RP-30A) in assessing left ventricular perfusion and function at rest and during exercise in coronary artery disease, and comparison with coronary arteriography and exercise thallium-2012 SPECT imaging. *Am J Cardiol* 1989; **64**: 270-5.

20. Baillet GY, Mena IG, Kuperus JH, Robertson JM, French WJ. Simultaneous technetium-99m MIBI angiography and myocardial perfusion imaging. *J Nucl Med* 1989; **30**: 38–44.

21. Najm YC, Timmis AD, Maisey MN, et al. The evaluation of ventricular function using gated myocardial imaging with Tc-99m MIBI. *Eur Heart J* 1989; **10**: 142-8.

22. Chua T, Kiat H, Germano G, et al. Gated technetium-99m sestamibi for simultaneous assessment of stress myocardial perfusion, postexercise regional ventricular function and myocardial viability – correlation with echocardiography and rest thallium-201 scintigraphy. *J Am Coll Cardiol* 1994; **23**: 1107-14.

23. Palmas W, Friedman JD, Kiat H, Silber H, Berman DS. Improved identification of multiple vessel coronary artery disease by addition of exercise wall motion analysis to technetium-99m sestamibi myocardial perfusion SPECT (abstract). *J Nucl Med* 1993; **34**: 130P.

24. DePuey EG, Jones ME, Garcia EV. Evaluation of right ventricular regional perfusion with technetium-99m sestamibi SPECT. *J Nucl Med* 1991; **32**: 1199-1205.

Pharmacological Stress Techniques

INTRODUCTION

The use of exercise for stress of the heart has been practised for over 60 years and clinicians are both familiar and comfortable with its use during exercise electrocardiography. However, no matter how well validated a technique, newer alternatives arise to challenge its use. This is the case with the pharmacological stress agents because many patients are unable to exercise to their full potential and a standard exercise stress test is then a suboptimal means for their assessment. The pharmacological stress agents largely remove the need for patient cooperation and motivation, and enable a confident assessment of cardiac function in virtually all cases. This has led to a great increase in their popularity.

ADENOSINE

Physiology

The use of adenosine for the detection of coronary artery disease is increasing and in time may supplant the use of dipyridamole. Adenosine (see Fig. 3) is a naturally occurring purine which mediates the cellular action of dipyridamole and can be given intravenously for a direct effect. It causes vasodilation by binding to the A2 receptor and increasing intracellular cyclic AMP (Fig. 1). Its main attraction is the very short half-life of between 2[1] and 10 s[2], which affords rapid control of the vasodilatation and any side-effects. The typical haemodynamic response to infusion of adenosine is a mild increase in heart rate, probably mediated by reflex response to peripheral vasodilatation, and a modest fall in systolic and diastolic blood pressure. The double product rises by a

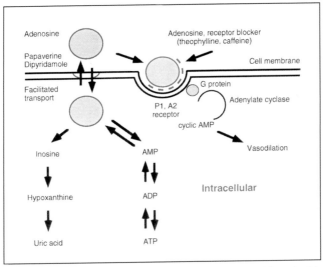

Fig. 1. *Cellular actions of adenosine on the A2 receptor. (Adapted with permission from Am J Cardiol 1991; 67: 12-17D)*

small amount. No significant difference has been demonstrated between the coronary hyperaemic response to adenosine and dipyridamole.[3,4] Near maximal coronary vasodilatation is achieved in 85% of patients with an intravenous dose of 140 µg/kg/min and the increase in coronary flow in humans at this dose is greater than 4 times baseline. A myocardial perfusion agent is injected in the third or fourth minute of the infusion. The flow reserve is reduced in arteries with fixed stenoses[5] and the differential flow between territories served by normal and by stenosed arteries may be sufficient to produce an apparent defect of thallium uptake. Ischaemia may also occur and the mechanisms for this are complex. First, increased flow across a stenosis reduces distal perfusion pressure, which may cause subendocardial ischaemia; second, flow is redirected to the subepicardium away from the subendocardium in myocardium supplied by a stenosed vessel;[5] third, flow in high-resistance collateral vessels serving the area of a diseased artery may be reduced because of the generalised vasodilation and fall in perfusion pressure.[6]

Symptoms caused by adenosine infusion

Symptoms are very common (80%) with adenosine infusion,[7] but they are short-lived and aminophylline, which competitively inhibits the action of adenosine on the purinoceptor,[8] is rarely needed. Side-effects are similar to those with dipyridamole, but the rapid onset of action and the higher plasma adenosine levels with direct infusion intensify the effects. Chest pain occurs in 30% but it is of limited diagnostic value because of its frequent occurrence in normal subjects.[9,10] Other symptoms include headache (21%), dyspnoea (19%), throat and epigastric pain (9% each), nausea (5%), dizziness (5%), sour taste (3%) and pains in other sites.[7]

Side-effects and contraindications

Adenosine exerts electrophysiological effects by binding to the A1 receptor. (Table 1). Atrioventricular conduction is inhibited, occasionally causing heart block (1° in 9%, 2° in 3% and 3° in 0.1%). Pre-existing high-degree heart block without a pacemaker is therefore a contraindication to adenosine,

Actions	Effects
Open potassium channels	Hyperpolarization
Block calcium channels	Inhibitory effects
Sino-atrial node	Increased cycle length, SA exit block, Shift of pacemaker of crista terminalis
Atrium	Reduction in atrial refractoriness
Atrio-ventricular node	Slows conduction (prolonged AH interval) AV block
WPW	Little effect
Ventrical	Little effect

Table 1 *Cellular actions of adenosine on the A1 receptor: mediation of electrophysiological effects*

although this rarely occurs. There is no evidence that pre-existing first-degree heart block progresses to higher grade block with adenosine.[7] If first-degree heart block occurs de novo, however, 25% will progress and care is necessary. Heart block during adenosine infusion is usually asymptomatic and responds to stopping of the infusion,[11] but patients with sino-atrial disease are at risk because of unusual sensitivity to the action of adenosine on sino-atrial function.[12] Sinus bradycardia[13] may result, which can progress to sinus arrest.[14] An exaggerated response is also seen in patients treated with dipyridamole, because of inhibition of adenosine deaminase. Dipyridamole should be stopped at least 12 h prior to adenosine infusion; otherwise very low doses with titration to patient symptoms must be used.

Adenosine is also contraindicated in asthma. Inhaled adenosine causes bronchoconstriction in asthmatic but not normal airways,[15] and may be a mediator of asthma.[16] After inhalation of adenosine, specific airways conductance falls, reaching a nadir of -45% at 5 min with a slow recovery.[15] Bronchoconstriction occurs in allergic and non-allergic asthmatic subjects though non-allergic subjects are less sensitive.[15] Intravenous adenosine also causes severe bronchospasm.[17] Therefore if asthmatic patients are unable to exercise, the correct alternative is to use dobutamine, which has been shown to be very safe in asthma.[18]

Caffeine[19,20,21] and treatment with methylxanthines[22] interfere with the action of adenosine by competitively inhibiting the A2 receptor (see Fig. 2 for structures of caffeine and theophylline). This occurs with low normal doses of these compounds.[23] Caffeine has a half-life of 5-7 h and should be avoided for at least 12 h prior to the study, and methylxanthines should be avoided for at least 24 h.

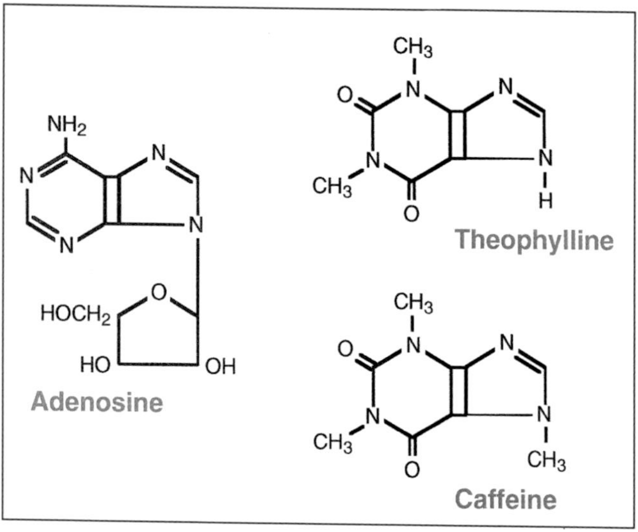

Fig 2 *Chemical structures of adenosine, theophylline and caffeine*

Safety

Single-centre studies and clinical experience suggest a good safety record with adenosine. There have been no published myocardial infarctions or deaths associated with adenosine in over 2400 patient studies, although two cardiac arrests have occurred in patients with covert sino-atrial disease.[14]

Clinical imaging results

Adenosine has been studied mainly for use with thallium myocardial perfusion imaging and has shown excellent results compared with coronary angiography[24,25,26,27] and exercise thallium imaging.[28,29,30,31] Adenosine is also useful for assessing left bundle branch block.[32]

DIPYRIDAMOLE

Physiology

Dipyridamole increases interstitial levels of adenosine by the combined effects of inhibition of the facilitated uptake of adenosine and inhibition of its breakdown by adenosine deaminase. This increases intracellular cAMP causing arteriolar vasodilatation.[33] The increase in coronary flow in humans using Gould's original canine regime of 0.56 mg/kg intravenous dipyridamole over 4 min[34] is between 2.5 and 6.0 times baseline.[35]

The increase in coronary flow after dipyridamole reaches its zenith approximately 2 min after the end of infusion,[35,36] when a myocardial perfusion agent should be given. The hyperaemic response is prolonged and the half-life of reduction in coronary flow is approximately 30 min;[37] therefore side-effects and ischaemia may be prolonged. These are reversed by aminophylline, but side-effects may re-emerge later. Caffeine[38,39] and treatment with methylxanthines[40] have been shown to interfere with the coronary hyperaemia and must be avoided prior to study.

Clinical imaging infusion protocol

Dipyridamole can be given either orally (400 mg) or intravenously at a standard dose (0.56 mg/kg), or at higher doses when used with echocardiography (0.841 mg/kg). Because gastric absorption of dipyridamole is very variable, plasma levels after an oral dose are unpredictable and the time of maximum coronary flow is unknown.[41] This makes oral administration unreliable for the production of perfusion abnormalities and it leads to a higher incidence of unpleasant gastrointestinal side–effects.[42] Intravenous administration is therefore preferred.

Symptoms caused by dipyridamole

The non-cardiac side-effects of dipyridamole are very similar to those described for adenosine, though they tend to be less intense because of the slower onset of hyperaemia. Following intravenous dipyridamole, chest pain occurs in 20% of patients, headache in 12%, dizziness in 12% and nausea in 5%.[43] Other side-effects are less common and mild.

Side-effects and contraindications

Minor dysrhythmias after dipyridamole are common, with the incidence of ventricular premature beats reported to be between 5%[43] and 20%.[44] Other dysrhythmias are rare, with reports of symptomatic bradycardia,[45] atrial fibrillation,[46] ventricular tachycardia[47] and ventricular fibrillation.[47,48] Bronchospasm after dipyridamole occurs in asthmatic patients.[49,50] One severe case and six less serious cases of bronchospasm after dipyridamole were reported in one series,[43] and eight cases in another,[47] with some of these patients and others[51] requiring intubation. Existing treatment with steroids does not appear to protect patients.[47] Therefore a history of asthma should be considered a contraindication to the use of dipyridamole, and dobutamine has been shown to be an effective alternative.[18] Other rare but serious complications with dipyridamole stress include stroke[52] and transient ischaemic attacks,[47] which may be related to reduced cerebral perfusion from hypotension or steal.

Safety

The safety of intravenous dipyridamole is good.[44,53,54] In a study of 3911 patients, one patient (0.026%) with chronic stable angina suffered myocardial infarction within 24 h of the dipyridamole infusion. A further three patients (0.077%) with unstable angina also had a myocardial infarction and two of the patients (0.051%) died. In another study, 170 patients with known or suspected unstable angina received dipyridamole infusion resulting in two infarctions (1.2%) but no deaths.[47] It is not possible to conclude that the infarctions were caused by dipyridamole, but dipyridamole in such patients was associated with increased risk. A study of 64000 patients undergoing dipyridamole testing has recently been presented in which the incidence of cardiac deaths was 0.01% and that of non-fatal myocardial infarction, 0.02%.[55]

The safety of a higher dose dipyridamole protocol (0.84 mg/kg) has been reviewed in 10451 studies.[56] Major complications occurred in seven patients (0.07%) and included one death, two myocardial infarctions, and prolonged ventricular tachycardia, pulmonary oedema and ventricular asystole in one patient each. Hypotension or bradycardia requiring aminophylline treatment was seen in 0.4%. These figures are not substantially different from those published for the standard dose dipyridamole protocol. No increase in serious complications has been reported using oral dipyridamole.[54]

Clinical imaging results

The first clinical trial used intravenous dipyridamole with thallium myocardial perfusion imaging,[57] and comparisons with coronary angiography[58,59,60] have shown excellent results, with diagnostic equivalence in comparison with exercise stress.[61,62,63] Oral dipyridamole has also been used successfully.[64] Comparison of the diagnostic potential of the intravenous and oral protocols shows similar results.[65] Comparison of submaximal stress and dipyridamole for thallium imaging has shown improved results with dipyridamole, suggesting that vasodilators should be used where suspicion of poor exercise tolerance exists.[66] Dipyridamole thallium imaging has also been shown to be useful in defining prognosis in stable angina,[67] before non-cardiac surgery,[68,69] after myocardial infarction,[70,71] in the elderly,[72] and in renal disease.[73]

DOBUTAMINE

Choice of ß-agonist and physiology

The ß-agonists (Fig. 3) increase myocardial oxygen demand through a combined inotropic and chronotropic action. Dobutamine is produced in a neutral non-irritant solution and it is the only commonly available inotrope for safe peripheral infusion. Dobutamine also causes significantly less dysrhythmia than the other inotropes in the ischaemic heart (Fig. 4),[74] a property also described in the human ischaemic heart.[75,76] Dobutamine has been shown to increase oxygen demand above availability,[77] but it also has other effects which contribute to the provocation of myocardial ischaemia. It dilates the distal coronary vessels, which leads to an increase in coronary flow[78,79,80] and a fall in perfusion pressure distal to coronary stenoses. Flow therefore becomes heterogeneous[81] and

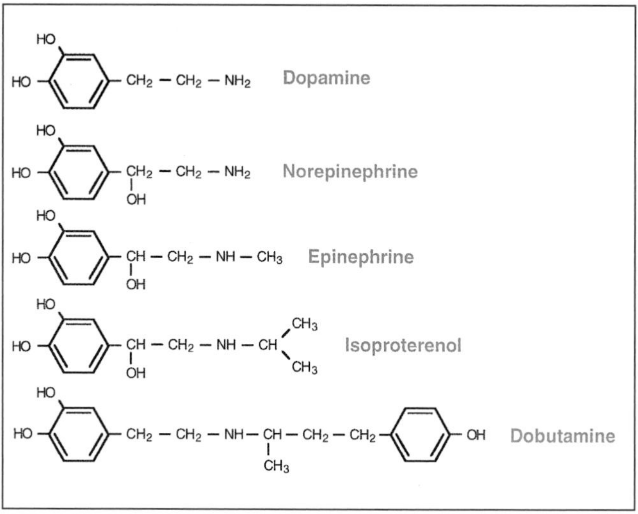

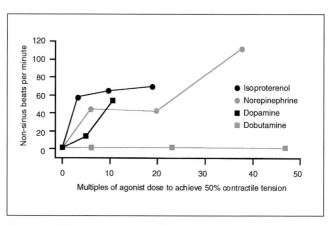

Fig. 3. *Structures of the common ß-agonists*

Fig. 4. *Arrhythmogenicity caused by ß-agonists measured as the number of non-sinus beats per minute.*
(Reproduced with permission[74])

may be redirected to the subepicardium.[78] Dobutamine may also increase flow resistance at the site of a stenosis.[78] The increase in coronary flow with dobutamine is not well studied but has been reported as 2.1 times baseline for an intermediate dose of 10 µg/kg/min.[78] A recent PET study suggests an increase of 2.9 times baseline at 40 µg/kg/min.[82] Dobutamine has a rapid onset and cessation of action (plasma half-life 120 s) allowing easy control of blood levels over any duration of imaging.

Imaging infusion protocol

Dobutamine has proved useful as an alternative to both exercise and the vasodilators. Dobutamine is given as an infusion and there is no accepted protocol for this at present. Doses up to 40 µg/kg/min have been used safely and a possible protocol compromising between allowing equilibrium at each stage of stress and the length of the stress might be to commence at 10 µg/kg/min and proceed in 10 µg/kg/min steps every 3 min. If patients have a poor chronotropic response to the dobutamine stress, atropine in doses from 0.25 to 1 mg improves diagnostic accuracy.[83]

Symptoms caused by dobutamine

Non-cardiac symptoms caused by dobutamine include tingling, flushing, nausea, headache, shaking and lightheadedness,[84] which, in general, are related to activation of the sympathetic nervous system.

Side-effects and contraindications

Non-sustained ventricular tachycardia occurs in about 4% of patients but is usually well tolerated.[85] Supraventricular tachycardia and atrial fibrillation may also occur. Ventricular and atrial premature beats are common, occurring in approximately 15% and 10% respectively. Other cardiac-related symptoms include pounding, palpitation and dyspnoea. Hypotension may occur during dobutamine infusion, but this may relate to intraventricular obstruction[86] and is not associated with the same adverse prognosis as when it is seen during dynamic exercise.[87] Dobutamine is contraindicated in the same conditions that apply to dynamic exercise, but is safe in asthma.[18]

Safety

The safety of dobutamine stress for thallium imaging has not been assessed but one study of its use for echocardiography in over 1000 patients with known or suspected coronary artery disease was not associated with myocardial infarctions, deaths or other serious sequelae.[85]

Clinical imaging results

Dobutamine has been used for thallium[18,84,88,89,90] and MIBI[91] myocardial perfusion imaging, with excellent results in comparison with coronary angiography and exercise stress. Dobutamine has also been used with thallium imaging[92] to determine the risk of surgery, and at low dose levels it may identify viable myocardium by increasing wall thickening in asynergic areas.[93]

COMPARISONS BETWEEN THE PHARMACOLOGICAL STRESS AGENTS

There are few direct comparisons of the stress agents involving nuclear medicine studies. A recent comparison of adenosine and dobutamine for both MIBI SPET and echocardiography showed equivalence for the two agents for MIBI, but poor sensitivity using adenosine for echocardiography.[94]

COMBINED VASODILATOR AND EXERCISE STRESS

The vasodilators have an excellent record in assessing coronary artery disease but suffer from several minor disadvantages. These include the level of troublesome side-effects and the high splanchnic thallium uptake, which may interfere with image interpretation. It has been shown that both of these problems can be resolved with the addition of moderate exercise to the vasodilator protocol. This would typically be 50-75 W on the bicycle ergometer. This has been demonstrated for both dipyridamole[95,96,97] and adenosine,[98,99], and for both drugs a trend towards improved diagnostic performance may be seen when the additional exercise is used. In the case of adenosine, it has also been shown that there is a significant reduction in dysrhythmias such as heart block with the added exercise.[99]

CONCLUSION

Exercise stress remains the technique of choice for evaluation of the cardiovascular system by nuclear medicine techniques, because it provides extra information such as the exercise duration and symptoms. In addition the electrocardiographic changes may be useful. However, there are a large number of patients whose exercise tolerance is suboptimal, and in clinical practice, patients who are difficult to assess because of physical or psychological limitations are commonly referred for nuclear medicine procedures. The stress agent of first choice in all these cases will be adenosine if it is available, and infusion should be coupled with mild to moderate exercise to limit side-effects and dysrhythmias. This technique is fast and requires little patient cooperation. It is also reasonable to use adenosine with exercise stress in all patients when the exercise tolerance has already been established by exercise electrocardiography. Dobutamine should be used in patients with asthma.

Acknowledgement

This chapter first appeared as: Pharmacological stress testing. Pennell DJ. In: Myocardial perfusion imaging, an update. *The Medicine Publishing Foundation series,* number 34. The Medicine Group, Oxford, UK. 1994: 27-34.

References

1. Möser GH, Schrader J, Deussen A. Turnover of adenosine in plasma of human and dog blood. *Am J Physiol* 1989; **256**: C799-806.

2. Klabunde RE. Dipyridamole inhibition of adenosine metabolism in human blood. *Eur J Pharmacol* 1983; **93**: 21-6.

3. Rossen JD, Quillen JE, Lopez AG, Stenberg RG, Talman CL, Winniford MD. Comparison of coronary vasodilation with intravenous dipyridamole and adenosine. *J Am Coll Cardiol* 1991; **18**: 485-91.

4. Chan SY, Brunken RC, Czernin J, Porenta G, Kuhle W, Krivokapich J, Phelps ME, Schelbert HR. Comparison of maximal myocardial blood flow during adenosine infusion with that of intravenous dipyridamole in normal men. *J Am Coll Cardiol* 1992; **20**: 979-85.

5. Feldman RL, Nichols WW, Pepine CJ, Conti CR. Acute effects of intravenous dipyridamole on regional coronary haemodynamics and metabolism. *Circulation* 1981; **64**: 333-44.

6. Chambers CE. Brown KA. Dipyridamole induced ST segment depression during thallium-201 imaging in patients with coronary artery disease: angiographic and haemodynamic determinants. *J Am Coll Cardiol* 1988; **12**: 37-41.

7. Abreu A, Mahmarian JJ, Nishimura S, Boyce TM, Verani MS. Tolerance and safety of pharmacologic coronary vasodilation with adenosine in association with thallium–201 scintigraphy in patients with suspected coronary artery disease. *J Am Coll Cardiol* 1991; **18**: 730-5.

8. Curnish RR, Berne RM, Rubio R. Effect of aminophylline on myocardial reactive hyperemia. *Proc Soc Exp Biol Med* 1972; **141**: 593-8.

9. Sylven C, Beermann B, Jonzon B, Brandt R. Angina pectoris like pain provoked by intravenous adenosine in healthy volunteers. *Br Med J* 1986; **293**: 227-30.

10. Sylven C, Borg G, Brandt R, Beermann B, Jonzon B. Dose effect relationship of adenosine provoked angina pectoris like pain - a study of the psychophysical power function. *Eur Heart J* 1988; **9**: 87-91.

11. Lee J, Heo J, Ogilby JD, Cave V, Iskandrian B, Iskandrian AS. Atrioventricular block during adenosine thallium imaging. *Am Heart J* 1992; **123**: 1569-73.

12. Watt AH. Sick sinus syndrome: an adenosine mediated disease. *Lancet* 1985; i: 786-8.

13. Benedini G, Cuccia C, Bolognesi R, Affatato A, Gallo G, Renaldi E, Visioli O. Value of purinic compounds in assessing sinus node dysfunction in man: a new diagnostic method. *Eur Heart J* 1984; **5**: 394-403.

14. Pennell DJ, Mahmood S, Ell PJ, Underwood SR. Bradycardia and cardiac arrest during adenosine thallium myocardial perfusion imaging in covert sino-atrial disease. *Eur J Nucl Med* 1994; **21**: 170-2.

15. Cushley MJ, Tattersfield AE, Holgate ST. Inhaled adenosine and guanosine on airway resistance in normal and asthmatic subjects. *Br J Clin Pharmacol* 1983; **15**: 161-5.

16. Holgate ST, Mann JS, Cushley MJ. Adenosine as a bronchoconstrictor mediator in asthma and its antagonism by methylxanthines. *J Allergy Clin Immunol* 1984; **74**: 302-6.

17. Taviot B, Pavheco Y, Coppere B, Pirollet B, Rebaudet P, Perrin-Fayolle M. Bronchospasm induced in an asthmatic by the injection of adenosine. *Presse Med* 1986; **15**: 1103.

18. Pennell DJ, Underwood SR, Ell PJ. Safety of dobutamine stress for thallium myocardial perfusion tomography in patients with asthma. *Am J Cardiol* 1993; **71**: 1346-50.

19. Smits P, Boekema P, de Abreu R, Thien T, Laar van't A. Evidence for an antagonism between caffeine and adenosine in the human cardiovascular system. *J Cardiovasc Pharmacol* 1987; **10**: 136-43.

20. Fredholm BB, Persson CGA. Xanthine derivatives as adenosine receptor antagonists. *Eur J Pharmacol* 1982; **81**: 673-6.

21. Smits P, Schouten J, Thien T. Cardiovascular effects of two xanthines and the relation to adenosine antagonism. *Clin Pharm Ther* 1989; **45**: 593-9.

22. Alfonso S. Inhibition of coronary vasodilating action of dipyridamole and adenosine by aminophylline in the dog. *Circ Res* 1970; **26**: 743-52.

23. Sollevi A, Ostergren J, Fagrell B, Hjendahl P. Theophylline antagonises cardiovascular responses to dipyridamole in man without affecting increases in plasma adenosine. *Acta Physiol Scand* 1984; **121**: 167-71.

24. LaManna MM, Mohama R, Slavich IL. Lumia FJ, Cha SD, Rambaran N, Maranhao V. Intravenous adenosine (Adenoscan) versus exercise in the non-invasive assessment of coronary artery disease by SPECT. *Clin Nucl Med* 1990; **15**: 804-5.

25. Verani MS, Mahmarian JJ, Hixson JB, Boyce TM, Staudacher RA. Diagnosis of coronary artery disease by controlled coronary vasodilation with adenosine and thallium-201 scintigraphy in patients unable to exercise. *Circulation* 1990; **82**: 80-7.

26. Nishimura S, Mahmarian JJ, Boyce TM, Verani MS. Equivalence between adenosine and exercise thallium-201 myocardial tomography: a multicenter, prospective, crossover trial. *J Am Coll Cardiol* 1992; **20**: 265-75.

27. Mahmarian JJ, Pratt CM, Nishimura S, Abreu A. Verani MS. Quantitative adenosine T1-201 single photon emission computed tomography for the early assessment of patients surviving acute myocardial infarction. *Circulation* 1993; **87**: 1197-1210.

28. Nguyen T, Heo J, Ogilby D, Iskandrian AS. Single photon emission computed tomography with thallium-201 during adenosine induced coronary hyperaemia: correlation with coronary arteriography, exercise thallium imaging and two-dimensional echocardiography. *J Am Coll Cardiol* 1990; **16**: 1375-83.

29. Coyne EP, Belvedere DA, Van de Streeke PR, Weiland FL, Evans RB, Spaccavento LJ. Thallium-201 scintigraphy after intravenous infusion of adenosine compared with exercise thallium testing in the diagnosis of coronary artery disease. *J Am Coll Cardiol* 1991; **17**: 1289-94.

30. Nishimura S, Mahmarian JJ, Boyce TM, Verani MS. Quantitative thallium-201 single photon emission computed tomography during maximal pharmacologic coronary vasodilation with adenosine for assessing coronary artery disease. *J Am Coll Cardiol* 1991; **18**: 736-45.

31. Gupta NC, Esterbrooks DJ, Hilleman DE, Mohiuddin SM. Comparison of adenosine and exercise thallium-201 single photon emission computed tomography (SPECT) myocardial perfusion imaging. *J Am Coll Cardiol* 1992; **19**: 248-57.

32. O'Keefe JH, Bateman TM, Silvestri R, Barnhart C. Safety and diagnostic accuracy of adenosine thallium-201 scintigraphy in patients unable to exercise and those with left bundle branch block. *Am Heart J* 1992; **124**: 614-21.

33. Szegi J, Szentmiklosi AJ, Cseppento A. On the action of specific drugs influencing the adenosine induced activation of cardiac purinoceptors. In: Papp JG, Ed. *Cardiovascular pharmacology 1987: results, concepts and perspectives.* Budapest: Akademiai Kiado; 1987; 591-9.

34. Gould KL. Noninvasive assessment of coronary stenoses by myocardial perfusion imaging during pharmacologic coronary vasodilatation. 1. Physiologic basis and experimental validation. *Am J Cardiol* 1978; **41**: 267-78.

35. Wilson RF, Laughlin DE, Ackell PH et al. Transluminal, subselective measurement of coronary artery blood flow velocity and vasodilator reserve in man. *Circulation* 1985; **72**: 72-92.

36. Wilson RF, White CW. Intracoronary papaverine: an ideal coronary vasodilator for studies of the coronary circulation in conscious humans. *Circulation* 1986; **73**: 444-51.

37. Brown BG, Josephson MA, Petersen RD et al. Intravenous dipyridamole combined with isometric handgrip for near maximal coronary flow in patients with coronary artery disease. *Am J Cardiol* 1981; **48**: 1077-85.

38. Smits P, Aengevaeren WRM, Corstens FHM, Thien T. Caffeine reduced dipyridamole induced myocardial ischaemia. *J Nucl Med* 1989; **30**: 1723-6.

39. Smits P, Corstens FHM, Aengevaeren WRM, Wackers FJ, Thien T. False negative dipyridamole thallium-201 myocardial imaging after caffeine infusion. *J Nucl Med* 1991; **32**: 1538-41.

40. Daley PJ, Mahn TH, Zielonka JS, Krubsack AJ, Akhtar R, Bamrah VS. Effect of maintenance oral theophylline on dipyridamole thallium-201 myocardial imaging using SPECT and dipyridamole induced hemodynamic changes. *Am Heart J* 1988; **115**: 1185-92.

41. Segall GM, Davis MJ. Variability of serum drug level following a single oral dose of dipyridamole. *J Nucl Med* 1988; **29**: 1662-7.

42. Askut SV, Port S, Collier D et al. Dipyridamole thallium-201 imaging. Complications associated with oral and intravenous routes of administration. *Clin Nucl Med* 1988; **13**: 786-8.

43: Ranhosky A, Rawson J. The safety of intravenous dipyridamole thallium myocardial perfusion imaging. *Circulation* 1990; **81**: 1205-9.

44. Homma S, Gilliland Y, Guiney TE, Strauss H, Boucher CA. Safety of intravenous dipyridamole for stress testing with thallium imaging. *Am J Cardiol* 1987; **59**: 152-4.

45. Pennell DJ, Underwood SR, Ell PJ. Symptomatic bradycardia complicating the use of intravenous dipyridamole for thallium-201 myocardial perfusion imaging. *Int J Cardiol* 1990; **27**: 272-4.

46. Pennell DJ, Ell PJ. Atrial fibrillation after intravenous dipyridamole for thallium-201 myocardial perfusion imaging. *Eur J Nucl Med* 1992; **19**: 1064-5.

47. Zhu YY, Chung WS, Botvinick EH et al. Dipyridamole infusion scintigraphy: the experience with its application in one hundred seventy patients with known or suspected unstable angina. *Am Heart J* 1991; **121**: 33-43.

48. Bayliss J, Pearson M, Sutton GC. Ventricular dysrhythmias following intravenous dipyridamole during stress myocardial imaging. *Br J Radiol* 1983; **56**: 686.

49. Cushley MJ, Tallant N, Holgate ST. The effect of dipyridamole on histamine and adenosine induced bronchoconstriction in normal and asthmatic subjects. *Eur J Respir Dis* 1985; **67**: 185-92.

50. Crimi N, Palermo F, Oliveri R et al. Enhancing effect of dipyridamole inhalation on adenosine induced bronchospasm in asthmatic patients. *Allergy* 1988; **43**: 179-83.

51. Lette J, Cerino M, Laverdier M, Tremblay J, Prenovault J. Severe bronchospasm followed by respiratory arrest during dipyridamole-thallium imaging. *Chest* 1989; **95**: 1345-7.

52. Whiting JH, Datz FL, Gabor FV, Jones SR, Morton KA. Cerebrovascular accident associated with dipyridamole thallium-201 myocardial imaging: case report. *J Nucl Med* 1993; **34**: 128-30.

53. Lam JYT, Chaitman BR, Glaenzer M et al. Safety and diagnostic accuracy of dipyridamole-thallium imaging in the elderly. *J Am Coll Cardiol* 1988; **11**: 585-9.

54. Askut SV, Port S, Collier D et al. Dipyridamole thallium-201 myocardial imaging: complications associated with oral and intravenous routes of administration. *Clin Nucl Med* 1988; **13**: 281-7.

55. Lette J and the multicenter dipyridamole safety study. Safety of dipyridamole testing in 64,000 patients (abstract). *J Am Coll Cardiol* 1993; **21 (Suppl A)**: 207A.

56. Picano E, Marini C, Pirelli S et al. Safety of intravenous high-dose dipyridamole echocardiography. *Am J Cardiol* 1992; **70**: 252-8.

57. Albro PC, Gould KL, Westcott RJ et al. Noninvasive assessment of coronary stenoses by myocardial imaging during pharmacological coronary vasodilation. III. Clinical trial. *Am J Cardiol* 1978; **42**: 751-60.

58. Leppo J, Boucher CA, Okada RD, Newell JB, Strauss W, Pohost GM. Serial thallium-201 myocardial imaging after dipyridamole infusion: diagnostic utility in detecting coronary stenoses and relationship to regional wall motion. *Circulation* 1982; **66**: 649-57.

59. Schmoliner R, Dudczak R, Kronik G et al. Thallium-201 imaging after dipyridamole in patients with coronary multivessel disease. *Cardiology* 1983; **70**: 145-51.

60. Fransisco DA, Collins SM, Co RT, Ehrhardt JC, van Kirk OC, Marcus ML. Tomographic thallium-201 myocardial perfusion scintigrams after maximal coronary artery vasodilation with intravenous dipyridamole. *Circulation* 1982; **66**: 370-9.

61. Josephson MA, Brown BG, Hecht HS, Hopkins J, Pierce CD, Petersen RB. Noninvasive detection and localisation of coronary stenoses in patients: comparison of resting dipyridamole and exercise thallium-201 myocardial perfusion imaging. *Am Heart J* 1982; **103**: 1008-18.

62. Varma SK, Watson DD, Beller GA. Quantitative comparison of thallium-201 scintigraphy after exercise and dipyridamole in coronary artery disease. *Am J Cardiol* 1989; **64**: 871-7.

63. Wilde P, Walker P, Watt I, Rees JR, Davies ER. Thallium myocardial imaging: recent experience using a coronary vasodilator. *Clin Radiol* 1982; **33**: 43-50.

64. Homma S, Callahan RJ, Ameer B et al. Usefulness of oral dipyridamole suspension for stress thallium imaging without exercise in the detection of coronary artery disease. *Am J Cardiol* 1986; **57**: 503-8.

65. Taillefer R, Lette J, Phaneuf DC, Léveillé J, Lemire F, Essiambre R. Thallium-201 myocardial imaging during pharmacological coronary vasodilation: comparison of oral and intravenous administration of dipyridamole. *J Am Coll Cardiol* 1986; **8**: 76-83.

66. Young DZ, Guiney TE, McKusick KA, Okada RD, Strauss HW, Boucher CA. Unmasking potential myocardial ischemia with dipyridamole thallium imaging in patients with normal submaximal exercise thallium tests. *Am J Noninvas Cardiol* 1987; **1**: 11-14.

67. Hendel RC, Layden JJ, Leppo JA. Prognostic value of dipyridamole thallium scintigraphy for evaluation of ischemic heart disease. *J Am Coll Cardiol* 1990; 109-16.

68. Leppo J, Plaja J, Gionet M, Tumolo J, Paraskos JA, Cutler BS. Noninvasive evaluation of cardiac risk before elective vascular surgery. *J Am Coll Cardiol* 1987; **9**: 269-76.

69. Lette J, Waters D, Lapointe J, Gagnon A, Picard M, Cerino M, Kerouac M. Usefulness of the severity and extent of reversible perfusion defects during thallium dipyridamole imaging for cardiac risk assessment before noncardiac surgery. *Am J Cardiol* 1989; **64**: 276-81.

70. Leppo JA, O'Brien J, Rothendler JA, Getchell JD, Lee VW. Dipyridamole thallium-201 scintigraphy in the prediction of future cardiac events after acute myocardial infarction. *N Engl J Med* 1984, **310**: 1014-8.

71. Gimple LW, Hutter AM, Guiney TE, Boucher CA. Prognostic utility of predischarge dipyridamole thallium imaging compared to predischarge submaximal exercise electro-cardiography and maximal exercise thallium imaging after uncomplicated acute myocardial infarction. *Am J Cardiol* 1989; **64**: 1243-8.

72. Shaw L, Chaitman BR, Hilton TC et al. Prognostic value of dipyridamole thallium-201 imaging in elderly patients. *J Am Coll Cardiol* 1992; **19:** 1390-8.

73. Derfler K, Kletter K, Balcke P, Heinz G, Dudczak R. Predictive value of thallium-201 dipyridamole myocardial stress scintigraphy in chronic haemodialysis patients and transplant recipients. *Clin Nephrol* 1991; **36:** 192-202.

74. Tuttle RR, Mills J. Dobutamine, development of a new catecholamine to selectively increase cardiac contractility. *Circ Res* 1975; **36:** 185-96.

75. Sakamoto T, Yamada T. Haemodynamic effects of dobutamine in patients following open heart surgery. *Circulation* 1977; **55:** 525-33.

76. Leier CV, Heban PT, Huss P et al. Comparative systemic and regional haemodynamic effects of dopamine and dobutamine in patients with cardiomyopathic heart failure. *Circulation* 1978; **58:** 466-75.

77. willerson JT, Hutton I, Watson JT, Platt MR, Templeton GH. Influence of dobutamine on regional myocardial blood flow and ventricular performance during acute and chronic myocardial ischemia in dogs. *Circulation* 1976; **53:** 828-33.

78. Warltier DC, Zyvlowski M, Gross GJ, Hardman HF, Brooks HL. Redistribution of myocardial blood flow distal to a dynamic coronary arterial stenosis by sympathomimetic amines. Comparison of dopamine, dobutamine and isoproterenol. *Am J Cardiol* 1981; **48:** 269-79.

79. Vasu MA O'Keefe DD, Kapellakis GZ, Vezeridis MP, Jacobs ML, Daggett WM, Powell WJ. Myocardial oxygen consumption: effects of epinephrine, isoproterenol, dopamine, norepinephrine and dobutamine. *Am J Physiol* 1978; **235:** 237-41.

80. Fowler MB, Alderman EL, Oesterle SN, Derby G, Daughters GT, Stinson EB, Ingels NB, Mitchell RS, Miller DG. Dobutamine and dopamine after cardiac surgery: greater augmentation of myocardial blood flow with dobutamine. *Circulation* 1984; **70 (Suppl I):** 103-11.

81. Meyer SL, Curry GC, Donsky MS, Twieg DB, Parkey RW, Willerson JT. Influence of dobutamine on haemodynamics and coronary blood flow in patients with and without coronary artery disease. *Am J Cardiol* 1976; **38:** 103-8.

82. Krivokapich J, Huang SC, Schelbert HR. Assessment of the effects of dobutamine on myocardial blood flow and oxidative metabolism in normal human subjects using nitrogen-13 ammonia and carbon-11 acetate. *Am J Cardiol* 1993; **71**: 1351-6.

83. McNeill AJ, Fioretti PM, El-Said ME-S, Salustri A, Forster T, Roelandt JRTC. Enhanced sensitivity for detection of coronary artery disease by addition of atropine to dobutamine stress echocardiography. *Am J Cardiol* 1992; **70**: 41-6.

84. Pennell DJ, Underwood SR, Swanton RH, Walker JM, Ell PJ. Dobutamine thallium myocardial perfusion tomography. *J Am Coll Cardiol* 1991; **18**: 1471-9.

85. Mertes H, Sawada SG, Ryan T, Segar DS, Kovacs R, Foltz J, Feigenbaum H. Symptoms, adverse effects and complications associated with dobutamine stress echocardiography. Experience in 1118 patients. *Circulation* 1993; **88**: 15-9

86. Pellikke PA, Oh JK, Bailey KR, Nichols BA, Monahan KH, Tajik AJ. Dynamic intraventricular obstruction during dobutamine stress echocardiography: a new observation. *Circulation* 1992; **86**: 1429-32.

87. Rosamund TL, Vacek JL, Hurwitz A, Rowland AJ, Beauchamp GD, Crouse LJ. Hypotension during dobutamine stress echocardiography: initial description and clinical relevance. *Am Heart J* 1992; **123**: 403-7.

88. Mason JR, Palac RT, Freeman ML et al. Thallium scintigraphy during dobutamine infusion: nonexercise dependent screening test for coronary disease. *Am Heart J* 1984; **107**: 481-5.

89. Wallbridge DR, Tweddel AC, Martin W, Hutton I. A comparison of dobutamine and maximal exercise as stress for thallium scintigraphy. *Eur J Nucl Med* 1993; **20**: 319-23.

90. Hays JT, Mahmarian JJ, Cochran AJ, Verani MS. Dobutamine thallium-201 tomography for evaluating patients with suspected coronary artery disease unable to undergo exercise or vasodilator pharmacologic stress testing. *J Am Coll Cardiol* 1993; **21**: 1583-90.

91. Forster T, McNeill AJ, Salustri A. Reijs AEM, El-Said ME-S, Roelandt JRTC, Fioretti PM. Simultaneous dobutamine stress echocardiography and technetium-99m isonitrile single photon emission computed tomography in patients with suspected coronary artery disease. *J Am Coll Cardiol* 1993; **21**: 1591-6.

92. Elliott BM, Robison JG, Zellner JL, Hendrix GH. Dobutamine TI-201 imaging: assessing cardiac risks associated with vascular surgery. *Circulation* 1991; **84 (Suppl III):** 54-60.

93. Piérard LA, de Landsheere CM, Berthe C, Rigo P, Kulbertus HE. Identification of viable myocardium by echocardiography during dobutamine infusion in patients with myocardial infarction after thrombolytic therapy: comparison with positron emission tomography. *J Am Coll Cardiol* 1990; **15:** 1021-31.

94. Marwick T, Willemart B, D'Hondt AM, Baudhuin T, Wijns W, Detry JM, Melin J. Selection of the optimal nonexercise stress for the evaluation of ischemic regional myocardial dysfunction and malperfusion: comparison of dobutamine and adenosine using echocardiography and Tc-99m-MIBI single photon emission computed tomography. *Circulation* 1993; **87:** 345-54.

95. Casale PN, Guiney TE, Strauss W, Boucher C. Simultaneous low level treadmill exercise and intravenous dipyridamole stress thallium imaging. *Am J Cardiol* 1988, **62:** 799-802.

96. Stern S, Grenberg DI, Corne R. Effect of exercise supplementation on dipyridamole thallium-201 image quality. *J Nucl Med* 1991; **32:** 1559-64.

97. Verzijlbergen FJ, Vermeersch PHMJ, Laarman GJ, Ascoop CAPL. Inadequate exercise leads to suboptimal imaging. Thallium-201 myocardial perfusion imaging after dipyridamole combined with low-level exercise unmasks ischemia in symptomatic patients with non-diagnostic thallium-201 scans who exercise submaximally. *J Nucl Med* 1991; **32:** 2071-8.

98. Pennell DJ, Mavrogeni S, Forbat SM, Karwatowski SP, Underwood SR. Adenosine combined with exercise for T1–201 myocardial tomography improves imaging and reduces side-effects (abstract). *Br Heart J* 1993; **62.**

99. Pennell DJ, Mavrogeni S, Forbat SM, Karwatowski SP, Underwood SR. Adenosine combined with dynamic exercise for myocardial perfusion imaging. *J Am Coll Cardiol* 1995; in press.

Image Interpretation

RAW DATA REVIEW

Essential to image interpretation is the review of the planar images which form the raw data of the tomograms. Although these have low counts with only coarse detail, artefacts are most easily detected at this stage. A cine display of the planar images is usually performed and excessive lung uptake, patient motion during the acquisition,[1,2] and upward creep may be apparent.[3] Patient motion is an important source of artefactual abnormality in tomography, and it is always important to know if it has occurred. Whilst the stress study may not be repeated with thallium imaging, it is always possible to repeat studies that have used a technetium-based tracer. Upward creep is usually seen in stress images following exercise, with a rise in the mean position of the diaphragm and the heart and the reduction of pulmonary volumes during recovery. This can lead to an artefactual defect which is usually in the inferior wall, but sometimes also in the anterior wall. It is relatively rare to find this phenomenon after rest, and therefore a reversible perfusion defect may be simulated. If there is any doubt whether upward creep has occurred, then the planar images can be summed to show the outline of the heart moving cranially through the acquisition. Correction programs can be used to reduce this artefact. Other artefacts detected by reviewing the planar images are breast attenuation, and metallic objects in upper pockets.

TOMOGRAPHIC DISPLAY AND REORIENTATION

The tomograms are best reviewed on the computer screen, because film and paper reproduction are not reliable and slice

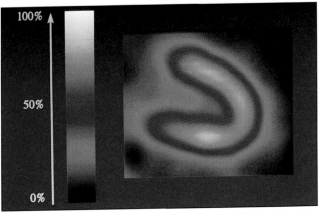

Fig. 1. *The colour scale used for images in this book. The white at the top of the scale is used to represent the pixels with the highest counts, and is set at 100% of activity. At the bottom of the scale, black represents zero counts and is set to 0% of activity. All pixels are then assigned a colour according to their relative counts to generate an image. Colour (and therefore count) normality depends on the normal regional distribution which is shown in Fig. 5, but in general orange and white always represent normal counts, whilst dark blue, green and black always represent reduced counts*

selection may not be ideal. A colour scale is used because it provides semiquantitative information on count distribution throughout the myocardium, and it also enhances the interpretation and presentation of the scans for non-experts. Familiarity with the colour scale is essential and it should be displayed on the screen and accompany all image reproductions (Fig. 1). Each image is displayed with the top and bottom colours of the scale representing the maximum and minimum number of counts in the voxels of the complete study. This ensures that different tomograms can be compared with each other.

Although it is possible to interpret the transaxial reconstructions directly, the anterior and inferior walls are sliced tangentially, which hinders interpretation, and comparisons between patients are also inhibited. Therefore it is normal to use reorientated views aligned to the long and short axes of the heart. The vertical long axis is defined from

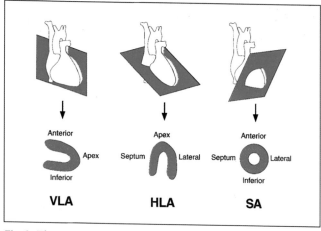

Fig. 2. *The reorientated tomographic planes are shown in relation to the surface projection of the heart. Whilst the surface projection varies widely from patient to patient, the planes reorientated to the long and short axes of the heart are very comparable between patients (reproduced with permission[40]). This makes consistent reading of the images much more straightforward. The walls of the heart are identified, and all the images in this book are reproduced in the identical format. The vertical long axis (VLA) is similar to a parasternal long-axis echocardiogram, the horizontal long axis (HLA) is similar to an apical four-chamber echocardiogram, and the short axis (SA) is similar to a parasternal short-axis echocardiogram*

the transaxial image allowing for the leftward deflection of the ventricle. The horizontal long axis is then defined from the downward inclination. The short-axis cuts are perpendicular to both of the long-axis views (Fig. 2). The most reproducible way to define both of the oblique angles is to place the cursor on the tip of the apex in each case, and define a line which then runs to the midpoint between the ends of the long walls. Image display as shown in all the images in this book is in accordance with the published guidelines.[4]

Whilst it is possible to directly compare all the images in the tomographic data sets on screen, there is a problem with displaying so many slices, which inevitably become rather small. For clinical purposes, most of the information is present in the central slices of the oblique planes and it is commonly possible to review the three planes in a four-quadrant screen display to examine these, with interactive manipulation of the slices. Comparison of the stress and rest studies can be made consecutively, or with an eight-quadrant screen with the corresponding views alongside.

QUALITATIVE TOMOGRAPHIC ANALYSIS

The myocardium is commonly divided into nine major segments, and whilst perfusion defects might occur which are smaller than this, the differences are not clinically significant. The nine segments consist of a basal and an apical portion of the four major walls (anterior, lateral, inferior, septum), and one segment for the apex. A defect can be described as mild if it involves one or two segments, moderate for three or four segments, and severe for five segments or more. The counts in each segment can be classified as normal, reduced (mild, moderate or severe) or absent. These categories reflect the counts as a percentage of maximum in the whole set of tomograms: i.e. 100%-70%, 70%-50%, 50%-30%, 30%-10% and 10%-0% respectively. For simple research purposes when a strictly quantitative analysis is not available or desirable, these categories can also be scored from 0 to 4 for each segment, which yields a 36-point scale of abnormality, with 0 reflecting normal and higher values reflecting increasingly severe ischaemia.[5] Clearly, a reduction in score between stress and redistribution imaging indicates reversibility.

NORMAL VARIATIONS

There is a wide variety of normal appearances arising from variation in size and position of the heart, body size, and quality of the tomographic acquisition.[6] Common variations in tracer distribution are summarised in Table 1. Knowledge of these and confidence in their identification is vital to prevent the reporting of defects when more experienced observers would correctly identify the scan as a normal variant.[7] An important issue to bear in mind if difficulty arises in distinguishing normal variants from true defects is that if the abnormality is only mild, the prognosis is very good and

Inferior attenuation

The inferior wall is further from the camera than the rest of the heart, and therefore the counts from this area are more attenuated. In addition, the inferior wall counts may be affected by respiratory motion. Inferior attenuation occurs more frequently in men, in whom normal inferior wall counts are 78% of maximum. The basal part of the inferior wall may be reduced to 50% of maximum. Upward creep also commonly affects the inferior wall preferentially.

Anterior attenuation

This commonly results from breast artefact. It is more common with large breasts, but clinical experience also suggests that smaller dense breasts may also cause problems, because of more discrete attenuation. Upward creep may also affect the anterior wall counts.

Apical thinning

The apical myocardium is thinner than elsewhere and counts may be reduced to at least 50% of maximum. In addition, the resolution characteristics of the camera are different for structures perpendicular or *en face* to the crystal, and this may manifest as reduced apical counts.

Short or attenuated septum

The basal part of the septum is membranous and does not take up thallium. Normal septal activity is lower than that of the lateral wall.

Lateral attenuation

Occasionally the lateral wall is attenuated by pendulous breasts in women or lateral fat pads in men.

Irregularity

Poor count statistics can lead to irregularity but this only rarely simulates the pattern of a perfusion defect.

Table 1 *Common normal variants of myocardial perfusion imaging*

therefore, as discussed later, it is wiser to err on the side of reporting the scan as normal.

If there is genuine doubt as to whether a defect is clinically significant, there are a number of manoeuvres which can be employed to assist the decision process. Repeat imaging in the prone position may help to identify inferior, breast and apical attenuation. For women, most centres now routinely strap the breasts, which yields similar results to prone imaging by creating more even attenuation across the anterior and lateral chest walls. A more recent innovation has been the use of gated imaging using the technetium agents, which is routinely possibly because of the high count rates. This can be performed as either a primary or a secondary procedure because of the prolonged residence time of the technetium agents in the heart. When an area of minor abnormality is shown to thicken and move normally, the likelihood that it represents artefactual attenuation of counts is considerably increased.[8]

Other features which aid interpretation are the clinical situation, the known coronary anatomy and a knowledge of the normal distribution of coronary perfusion. If the clinical question is whether ischaemia might be resulting from a stenosis of the proximal left anterior descending artery, then there is little point in expressing concern over inferior attenuation. Similarly, if a defect involves a known coronary territory, such as the septum, anterior wall and apex (left anterior descending artery), then it is almost certainly a true perfusion defect, whereas if it does not fit with normal coronary anatomy it is more likely to be artefactual.

ABNORMAL APPEARANCES IN CORONARY ARTERY DISEASE

The size and shape of the ventricle is important. It is difficult to gauge the size of the ventricle in absolute terms, but dilation which is present after stress which resolves after redistribution implies extensive reversible ischaemia and an adverse prognosis.[9] Wall thickening with hypertrophy may sometimes be apparent. Divergence of the anterior and inferior walls may suggest an apical aneurysm. The normal right ventricle is usually seen after stress, but is much better viewed with technetium agents than thallium.[10] If the right ventricle is hypertrophied it may take up almost as much tracer as the left ventricle.

Abnormalities of perfusion are usually classified as either fixed or reversible, indicating infarcted and reversibly ischaemic myocardium respectively. This simplification is a useful guide, but in practice redistribution is often incomplete when perfusion is low, for example when an occluded artery is present. Redistribution imaging at 3-4 h may then underestimate the amount of myocardium present in a region, and consequently underestimate reversibility. Later imaging or reinjection helps to achieve a more accurate impression of the myocardial mass still present in such regions.[11,12] The issues of hibernation and the accurate assessment of myocardial mass within a region showing a perfusion defect are dealt with in the chapter on hibernation. It is also relevant to note that mixed patters of fixed and reversible defects may occur, and this is more common in the thrombolytic era with partial infarction occurring as the result of successful reperfusion after occlusion. Another less common pattern of defect is reverse redistribution. This is applied to the occurrence of worsened relative counts on redistribution imaging compared with the stress images. Faster washout from this region compared with surrounding myocardium appears to be the cause. There is uncertainty over its significance but it certainly can occur following partial infarction with a patent coronary vessel,[13] and is quite common after thrombolysis.

ABNORMAL APPEARANCES IN OTHER DISEASES

Myocardial perfusion defects indicate inhomogeneous tracer delivery to the myocardium or variable uptake. This may occur in a number of unusual diseases (Table 2), but it is often not possible to assign clinical significance to these findings. These defects are often fixed but reversible defects may also occur. There are two conditions in which the defects are of greater clinical importance: left bundle branch block and hypertrophic cardiomyopathy.

Left bundle branch block is not uncommon in the cardiology clinic and it precludes assessment of the ST segments during exercise electrocardiography. Patients with left bundle branch block are therefore commonly referred for myocardial perfusion imaging to determine whether the conduction defect is associated with coronary artery disease. This can prove quite difficult to sort out, and experience is required to prevent inappropriate reporting. The first rule is that exercise should not be used for the stress, but adenosine or dipyridamole alone. The second rule is that if the stress images are normal, coronary artery disease is very unlikely. The third rule is that if reversible ischaemia is identified, then interpretation must be guarded.

The problems occur because in left bundle branch block, the duration of diastolic coronary flow is shortened in the septum by delayed relaxation, which results in inadequate diastolic coronary flow during tachycardia.[14] Reversible perfusion defects can be obtained in the absence of coronary artery

Large coronary arteries
Coronary artery spasm[33]
Coronary artery anomalous origin
Muscle bridging[34]
Small coronary vessel disease
Diabetes
SyndromeX[35]
Muscle disease
Hypertrophic cardiomyopathy[36,37]
Dilated cardiomyopathy
Ventricular hypertrophy
Infiltration
Amyloidosis
Sarcoidosis[38]
Connective tissue disease[39]
Left bundle branch block

Table 2 *Conditions other than coronary artery disease associated with perfusion defects*

disease by this mechanism alone. It is important to remember that the myocardial perfusion study is being used clinically, in the vast majority of cases, to determine whether catheterisation is required for significant coronary artery disease, and not for the identification of functional ischaemia. It is therefore very important to keep the heart rate low during stress to keep the functional ischaemia to a minimum, and exercise must be avoided. The incidence of studies which are "false-positive" for coronary artery disease can be considerably reduced in this way.[15,16] It is worth noting, however, that epicardial coronary artery disease still remains the commonest cause of thallium defects in patients with left bundle branch block.[17] Technetium agents may also have a role to play.[18]

The site of the defect can be helpful, because anterior and septal defects are much more likely to be the result of the conduction defect in the absence of coronary artery disease than defects in other areas. Like all rules, however, this does not apply in all cases, and the site of defect can vary. The explanation for the occurrence of fixed defects is not entirely clear but there are two possibilities: first, that infarction has occurred which has affected the left bundle, and this has resulted from an embolus or thrombosis on a minor plaque that is not easily identified by angiography; second, a slowly progressive or stable cardiomyopathy may be present.

Another recently described use of thallium imaging in non-coronary disease has shown that ischaemia is an important cause of sudden cardiac arrest or syncope in patients with hypertrophic cardiomyopathy.[19] This study is unusual because it suggests that ischaemia may be the primary cause of electrical instability in these patients' hearts. In addition, treatment with verapamil or ß-blockers improved regional thallium uptake and treatment was associated with fewer cardiac events.

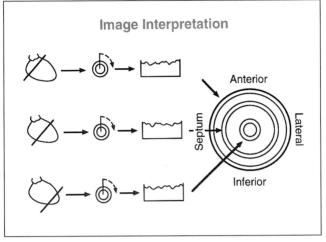

Fig. 3. *Reconstruction of the polar plot or "bullseye" image. The apical short-axis tomogram is laid down in the centre of a circular image with more basal slices appearing outside it. The resulting image has the effect of transforming the conical myocardium into a disk. (Reproduced with permission[40])*

IMAGE QUANTIFICATION

Visual analysis of the images is usually sufficient for assessment, but quantification of the tracer counts has merit because it improves interobserver and intraobserver variability, which makes the routine reports more consistent, and it is very useful in research to give an unbiased assessment of defect size and severity. Formal comparisons of quantitative and qualitative analysis suggests only a marginal clinical benefit for diagnosis with the more complex technique, however.[20,21,22,23] Many departments do not use quantification routinely, and high-quality clinical experience is, in most cases, quite satisfactory. Quantification may be helpful, however, in difficult cases, or as an adjunct to back up interpretation. Conversely, it must always be remembered that quantification would more appropriately be described as "semi-quantification in relation to a normal database", because normality is very difficult to define, attenuation correction is not yet routinely available, and all quantification schemes

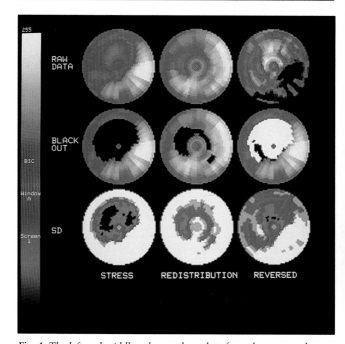

Fig. 4. *The left and middle columns show data from the stress and redistribution thallium acquisitions in a patient with severe anteroseptal and apical reversible ischaemia. The right column marked "reversed" is essentially a subtraction of the stress from the redistribution bullseye to show where activity has improved. The top row is the raw data plots, whilst the middle row shows areas on the bullseye as black, where activity is >2.5 standard deviations below that of a reference normal population. This is essentially therefore an "extent of perfusion defect" map. The bottom row shows the depth of abnormality as the number of standard deviations below the mean that the actual counts represent. More severe defects therefore show in darker colours such that green represents between 5-7 standard deviations below the mean, and black >7. This is essentially a "severity of defect" map. The reverse map in the middle row shows the original defect with the black pixels whitened where significant reversibility of the defect has occurred. Quantification of the defect is straightforward from these maps, by counting the number of abnormal pixels (size) and assessing the total summed number of standard deviations from the mean (severity). In this case 213 pixels were blacked out, and 188 (88%) showed reversibility. There were a total of 1292 summed standard deviations below the mean of which 773 reversed*

require a normal database which by necessity is limited in range of body habitus, racial and ethnic variability. Therefore defects which are only seen by quantification must be interpreted very cautiously.

The most commonly used quantification system is the bullseye or polar plot (Fig. 3), in which all areas of the myocardium are represented in a single image, by wrapping each successive short-axis image around the previous, starting from the apex.[24,25,26] The image can be used to show raw counts, areas of abnormality or reversibility, or washout (Fig. 4). The polar map is not straightforward to interpret because equal areas of myocardium are not mapped to equal areas of the polar plot and so the size of a defect becomes distorted. Furthermore, if stress and redistribution polar plots are to be compared, the mapping of both studies must be identical. However, the area of abnormal pixels and the relative depth of severity can be generated, which allows at least an unbiased measure of the severity of perfusion defect.

Because there is no simple relationship between tracer uptake and the number of counts in each voxel, the image is scaled relative to the pixel with maximum counts, as in the tomographic display. With improvements in attenuation correction, it may become possible for a more absolute type of display in the future, where absolute counts may be related to tracer concentration in the myocardium. At present, therefore, the normal distribution of tracer counts with thallium still relates to a myocardial maximum pixel, and in both men and women this occurs in the lateral wall. The regional and gender differences are shown in the normal counts polar maps in Fig. 5.[27] The lowest counts are seen in the inferior wall in men, and in the septum in women.

Another quantitative measure used for detection of ischaemia is washout analysis.[28] This is only really applicable to thallium, although it might also be possible with ^{99m}Tc-teboroxime. Following initial uptake of thallium, washout occurs from the myocardium, but in ischaemic areas the rate of washout is reduced because of the lower intracellular concentration, and in addition, cellular uptake is increased. This is the basis of redistribution, and a quantitative assessment of washout is

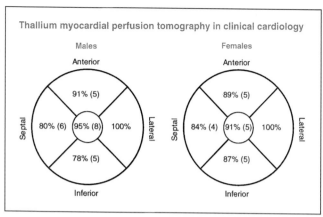

Fig. 5. *Polar maps showing the mean distribution of thallium after exercise in normal subjects. The lateral wall normally contains the highest activity and is scaled to 100% to allow a comparison with other territories. (Adapted with permission[27])*

akin to assessing redistribution directly. Analysis which shows a washout abnormality in the absence of redistribution, however, may well be artefactual and therefore the analysis adds little in practice.

LUNG UPTAKE OF THALLIUM

High uptake of thallium in the lungs is an important variable for the prediction of future cardiac events.[29,30] The factors which affect lung uptake include pulmonary transit time, extraction efficiency by the lungs, and pulmonary capillary pressure, and therefore increased uptake reflects poor left ventricular function at rest or during stress.[31] Lung uptake is usually expressed as a ratio between uptake in the lungs and the heart, which is measured from an initial anterior planar image or from the tomographic acquisition. Usually, regions of interest are placed over the entire right lung field and the whole of the heart. The upper limit in patients without coronary artery disease varies between 0.78 and 0.86.[32]

CONSERVATIVE REPORTING AND AUDIT

An important issue that should be in the mind of the person reporting a myocardial perfusion study is "What effect will this report have on the referring physician?". This has three components: Is the report conclusion relevant to the question being asked? What effect will this report have on the patient management? And, how can this report inspire confidence in the physician? It is all too easy for myocardial perfusion imaging reports to be produced in a clinical vacuum, and this inevitably leads to the opening of a confidence gap that inhibits both appropriate clinical referrals and sensible integration of the results in the scheme of patient management. Each department should critically audit its reporting of perfusion scans and what effect the report has on clinical management to ensure that confidence in the reports is high.

There are two common examples of where a breakdown in confidence occurs, and these may be specifically sought within the department. The first is usually straightforward, in that if more than a few percent of patients with normal myocardial perfusion scans are being catheterised, either the referring physician needs to be educated about the very low incidence of cardiac events in such patients, which nearly always makes angiography unnecessary, or the report has not made this clear. Such an audit requires very little effort, and may reveal that the reporting needs to be more definite in its conclusions. For example, from the referring cardiologist's point of view, there is a tremendous difference between a report which says "Normal myocardial perfusion with stress – This suggests a low likelihood of future cardiac events" and one which states "There is a mild fixed inferior wall defect which may be due to attenuation and there are probably no convincing changes elsewhere".

The second example concerns auditing of the number of normal coronary angiograms in patients in whom the thallium has been reported as abnormal, as this should also be very low. This is more contentious, because this usually directly implies that the nuclear cardiology department is at fault in throwing up too many false-positives, which can be a bitter pill to accept. This scenario, however, is one which referring cardiologists find instantly disagreeable, and if repeated more than just occasionally, is guaranteed to greatly reduce confidence and referrals. Once identified as a problem, the remedy comes in critically assessing two aspects of the study, namely the quality control of the acquisition and the quality control of the reporting. The scanning may be addressed with careful attention to detail and a systematic regular program of, for example, flood field uniformity and centre of rotation checks, which is best organised by the most capable member of the team, invariably the departmental physicist in the first instance. Once established in practice, the radiographer usually carries out the checks on a routine basis.

Unfortunately, the other side of the coin, changing habits of reporting, is usually very difficult. The best way forward if the number of false-positive reports is too high, is to sit down with the referring clinician and attempt to establish a pattern of where the problems lie. This is because there is often a lack of feedback between the cardiologist, who finds normal coronary angiography in a patient with a reportedly positive thallium scan, and the nuclear department. The cardiologist may swear under his breath, but may not have the time or the inclination to try to improve the situation. Any nuclear department starved of seeing the results of its errors is unlikely to provide a quality service.

One area where critical appraisal of reporting can be very valuable is with inferior wall attenuation, which is probably the single most common reporting problem. Take for example a case of an asymptomatic 90 kg, 45-year-old male driver with mild hypertension, who has a borderline positive exercise test at 14 min of the Bruce protocol, who is referred for myocardial perfusion imaging. The thallium scan shows a reduction in inferior wall counts which was unchanged between stress and redistribution. How is this to be reported? The pre-test likelihood of disease is low, and the nuclear physician should clearly have this in mind. Examination of the normal pattern of thallium activity in normal men shows that inferior wall counts are only 78% of those in the lateral wall. This figure is, however, an average, and in the larger patient the counts may be even lower than this. If in this case inferior wall counts were shown to be 70% of those in the lateral wall, it is not satisfactory at this stage to switch off clinically and simply report a "fixed inferior wall defect" in the hope that the cardiologist will ignore it. Such a report will almost certainly lead to catheterisation, which in all likelihood will be normal. The result of this report is that the cardiologist and patient are upset, and the nuclear report is derided. Likewise it is also not really satisfactory to report the scan as a "fixed inferior wall defect which is probably due to inferior wall attenuation". This still leaves the cardiologist having to make up his mind what to actually do to protect the driver (and his passengers), when he may be the least experienced person to interpret what inferior attenuation actually means! The correct report in this hypothetical example is to eschew equivocation, and state facts: "Myocardial perfusion is within normal limits", which is undoubtedly true; And, "There is a low likelihood of future cardiac events", which is also undoubtedly true and very relevant. These statements would be both accurate and helpful to the cardiologist, and certainly convey the correct conclusion which is that if there is any coronary disease present at all, it must be very mild. If he, too, is happy that there is no other clinical reason to continue to catheterisation, then he can avoid doing so with this report and from the clinical viewpoint this is appropriate. Therefore, the moral of the example is that equivocation and over-reporting are ruinous to referring physician confidence, and audit of departmental results as outlined above must be used to prevent this. Conservative reporting is to be preferred to over-reporting.

VLA   HLA   SA

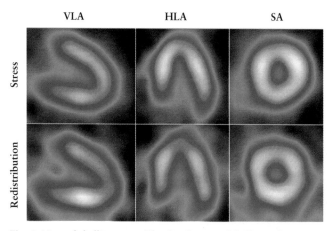

Fig. 6. *Normal thallium scan. The distribution of thallium after stress and after 4 hours redistribution is normal (note that the maximum counts per pixel were 120 after stress and 90 after redistribution)*

VLA   HLA   SA

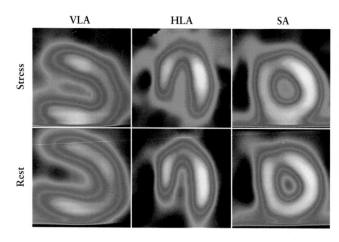

Fig. 7. *Normal tetrofosmin scan. The tracer distribution after the stress and rest injections (one day stress/rest protocol) is normal. Note the superior image quality which is related to the higher counts in the image (the maximum counts per pixel were 200 after stress and 700 after rest)*

72

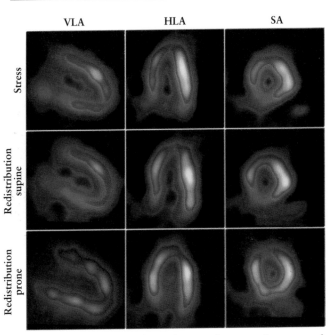

Fig. 8. *Inferior attenuation. This study in an obese man shows normal myocardial perfusion using thallium. There is inferior wall attenuation particularly affecting the basal inferior segment. This is common, especially in men, and is thought to be a result of increased attenuation of photons from the deeper inferior myocardium. Prone imaging alters the position of the heart and reduces this attenuation. Inferior wall attenuation is very common and care should be taken that it is not interpreted as abnormal, especially if there is no other reason to suspect disease (images reproduced with permission from Thallium myocardial perfusion tomography in clinical cardiology. Pennell, Underwood, Costa, Ell. Springer-Verlag, London 1992)*

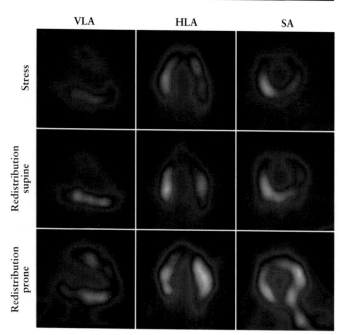

Fig. 9. *Anterior attenuation. This study shows normal myocardial perfusion in an obese woman using thallium, but there is significant anterior wall attenuation from large breasts which was apparent in the planar images. Prone imaging evens out the attenuation and helps to avoid the artefact. There was normal anterior wall motion and normal left ventricular ejection fraction with normal coronary arteries. Myocardial perfusion imaging with the ^{99m}Tc-agents suffers less from these attenuation problems because of the higher energy photon emission (images reproduced with permission from Thallium myocardial perfusion tomography in clinical cardiology. Pennell, Underwood, Costa, Ell. Springer-Verlag, London 1992)*

References

1. Cooper JA, Neumann PH, McCandless BK. Detection of patient motion during tomographic myocardial perfusion imaging. *J Nucl Med* 1993; **34**: 1341-8.

2. Germano G, Chua T, Kavanagh PB, Kiat H, Berman DS. Detection and correction of patient motion in dynamic and static myocardial SPECT using a multiheaded camera. *J Nucl Med* 1993; **34**: 1349-55.

3. Friedman J, Van Train K, Maddahi J, et al. "Upward creep" of the heart: a frequent source of false-positive reversible defects during the thallium-201 stress-redistribution SPECT. *J Nucl Med* 1989; **30**: 1718-22.

4. American College of Cardiology, American Heart Association, Society of Nuclear Medicine Policy Statement. Standardization of cardiac tomographic imaging. *Circulation* 1992; **86**: 338-9.

5. Pennell DJ, Mavrogeni S, Forbat SM, Karwatowski SP, Underwood SR. Adenosine combined with dynamic exercise for myocardial perfusion imaging. *J Am Coll Cardiol* 1995; in press.

6. DePuey EG, Garcia EV. Optimal specificity of thallium-201 SPECT through recognition of imaging artefacts. *J Nucl Med* 1989; **30**: 441-9.

7. DePuey EG. How to detect and avoid myocardial perfusion SPECT artifacts. *J Nucl Med* 1994; **35**: 699-702.

8. DePuey EG, Rozanski A. Gated Tc-99m sestamibi SPECT to characterize fixed defects as infarct or artifact (abstract). *J Nucl Med* 1992; **33**: 927.

9. Weiss AT, Berman DS, Lew AS, et al. Transient ischaemic dilatation of the left ventricle on stress thallium-201 scintigraphy: a marker of severe and extensive coronary artery disease. *J Am Coll Cardiol* 1987; **9**: 752-9.

10. DePuey EG, Jones ME, Garcia EV. Evaluation of right ventricular regional perfusion with technetium-99m sestamibi SPECT. *J Nucl Med* 1991; **32**: 1199-1205.

11. Cloninger KG, DePuey EG, Garcia EV, et al. Incomplete redistribution in delayed thallium-201 single photon emission computed tomographic (SPECT) images: an overestimation of myocardial scarring. *J Am Coll Cardiol* 1988; **12**: 955-63.

12. Ziessman HA, Keyes JW, Fox LM, Green CE, Fox SM. Delayed redistribution in thallium-201 SPECT myocardial perfusion studies. *Chest* 1989; **96**: 1031-5.

13. Weiss AT, Maddahi J, Lew AS, et al. Reverse redistribution of thallium-201: a sign of nontransmural myocardial infarction with patency of the infarct-related coronary artery. *J Am Coll Cardiol* 1986; **7**: 61-67.

14. Hirzel HO, Senn M, Nuesch K, et al. Thallium-201 scintigraphy in complete left bundle branch block. *Am J Cardiol* 1984; **53**: 764-9.

15. O'Keefe JH, Bateman TM, Barnhart CS. Adenosine thallium-201 is superior to exercise thallium-201 for detecting coronary artery disease in patients with left bundle branch block. *J Am Coll Cardiol* 1993; **21**: 1332-8.

16. Burns RJ, Galligan L, Wright LM, Lawand S, Burke RJ, Gladstone PJ. Improved specificity of myocardial thallium-201 single photon emission computed tomography in patients with left bundle branch block by dipyridamole. *Am J Cardiol* 1991; **68**: 504-8.

17. Jazmati B, Sadaniantz A, Emaus SP, Heller GV. Exercise thallium-201 imaging in complete left bundle branch block and the prevalence of septal perfusion defects. *Am J Cardiol* 1991; **67**: 46-9.

18. Notohamiprodjo G, Vyska K, Fassbender D, Schmidt U, Gleichmann U. Technetium-99m hexakis 2-methoxy-2-isobutylisonitrile myocardial scintigraphy for the noninvasive diagnosis of coronary artery disease in patients with complete left bundle branch block. *Am J Noninvasive Cardiol* 1993; **7**: 317-24.

19. Dilsizian V, Bonow RO, Epstein SE, Fananapazir L. Myocardial ischemia detected by thallium scintigraphy is frequently related to cardiac arrest and syncope in young patients with hypertrophic cardiomyopathy. *J Am Coll Cardiol* 1993; **3**: 796-804.

20. Maddahi J, Garcia EV, Berman DS, Waxman A, Swan HJC, Forrester J. Improved noninvasive assessment of coronary artery disease by quantitative analysis of regional stress myocardial distribution and washout of thallium-201. *Circulation* 1981; **64**: 924-35.

21. Francisco DA, Collins SM, Go RT, Ehrhardt JC, Van Kirk OC, Marcus ML. Tomographic thallium-201 myocardial perfusion scintigrams after maximal coronary artery vasodilation with intravenous dipyridamole. *Circulation* 1982; **66**: 370-9.

22. Tamaki NY, Yonekura T, Imkai T, et al. Segmental analysis of stress thallium myocardial emission tomography for localisation of coronary artery disease. *Eur J Nucl Med* 1984; **9**: 99-105.

23. Niemeyer MG, Laarman GJ, Lelbach S, et al. Quantitative thallium-201 myocardial exercise scintigraphy in normal subjects and patients with normal coronary arteries. *Eur J Radiol* 1990; **10**: 19-27.

24. Garcia EV, Van Train K, Maddahi J, et al. Quantitation of rotational thallium-201 myocardial perfusion tomography. *J Nucl Med* 1985; **26**: 17-26.

25. DePasquale EE, Nody AC, DePuey EG, et al. Quantitative rotational thallium-201 tomography for identifying and localising coronary artery disease. *Circulation* 1988; 77: 316-27.

26. Mahmarian JJ, Boyce TM, Goldberg RK, Cocanougher MK, Roberts R, Verani MS. Quantitative exercise thallium-201 single photon emission computed tomography for the enhanced diagnosis of ischaemic heart disease. *J Am Coll Cardiol* 1990; **15**: 318-29.

27. DePasquale EE, Nody AC, DePuey EG, et al. Quantitative rotational thallium-201 tomography for identifying and localising coronary artery disease. *Circulation* 1988; **77**: 316-27.

28. Leppo J. Thallium washout analysis: fact or fiction? *J Nucl Med* 1987; **28**: 1058-60.

29. Gill JB, Ruddy TD, Newell JB, et al. Prognostic importance of thallium uptake by the lungs during exercise in coronary artery disease. *N Engl J Med* 1987; **317**: 1485-9.

30. Kurata C, Tawarahara K, Taguchi T, Sakata K, Yamazaki N, Naitoh Y. Lung thallium-201 uptake during exercise emission computed tomography. *J Nucl Med* 1991; **32**: 417-23.

31. Mannting F. Pulmonary thallium uptake: correlation with systolic and diastolic left ventricular function at rest and during exercise. *Am Heart J* 1990; **119**: 1137-46.

32. Mannting F. A new method for quantification of pulmonary thallium uptake in myocardial SPECT studies. *Eur J Nucl Med* 1990; **16**: 213-22.

33. Ricci DR, Orlick AE, Doherty PW, Cipriano PR, Harrison DC. Reduction of coronary blood flow during coronary artery spasm occurring spontaneously and after provocation by ergonovine maleate. *Circulation* 1978; **57**: 392-5.

34. Bennett JM, Blomerus P. Thallium-201 scintigraphy perfusion defect with dipyridamole in a patient with a myocardial bridge. *Clin Cardiol* 1988; **11**: 268-70.

35. Meller J, Goldsmith SJ, Rudin A, et al. Spectrum of exercise thallium-201 myocardial perfusion imaging in patients with chest pain and normal coronary angiograms. *Am J Cardiol* 1979; **43**: 717-23.

36. O'Gara PT, Bonow RO, Maron BJ, et al. Myocardial perfusion abnormalities in patients with hypertrophic cardiomyopathy: assessment with thallium-201 emission computed tomography. *Circulation* 1987; **76**: 1214-23.

37. von Dohlen TW, Prisant LM, Frank MJ. Significance of positive or negative thallium-201 scintigraphy in hypertrophic cardiomyopathy. *Am J Cardiol* 1989; **64**: 498-503.

38. Bulkley BH, Rouleau JR, Whitaker JQ, Strauss HW, Pitt B. The use of thallium-201 for myocardial perfusion imaging in sarcoid heart disease. *Chest* 1977; **72**: 27-32.

39. Follansbee WP, Curtiss EI, Medsger TA, et al. Physiologic abnormalities of cardiac function in progressive systemic sclerosis with diffuse scleroderma. *N Engl J Med* 1984; **310**: 142-8.

40. Pennell DJ, Underwood SR, Costa DC, Ell PJ. Thallium myocardial perfusion tomography in clinical cardiology. *London: Springer;* 1992: P38.

Diagnosis in Coronary Artery Disease

CORONARY ANATOMY

When interpreting myocardial perfusion tomograms, it is often useful to comment on the localisation of disease to particular arterial territories, as this can be helpful as a guide to angioplasty for example, but it is important to note that the distribution of the coronary arteries is variable. The most constant vessel is the left anterior descending artery, which supplies the distal anterior wall and apex, with septal and diagonal branches supplying the septum and proximal anterior wall (Fig. 1). A proximal left anterior descending lesion may therefore cause a defect of the whole of the anterior wall, apex and septum, or it may spare the septum or basal anterior wall if septal or diagonal branches are spared. It is unusual for a defect to involve the septum without the anterior wall. A large left anterior descending artery may extend around the apex to perfuse the inferior wall, and therefore occasionally it can be difficult to distinguish a proximal stenosis in a large left anterior descending artery from two-vessel disease also involving the right coronary artery. Conversely, the inferior portion of the septum may be supplied by the posterior descending artery arising from the right or circumflex arteries.

In 85% of people the right coronary artery is dominant, meaning that it gives rise to the posterior descending artery, which supplies the inferior and inferoseptal walls, and in the other 15% the left circumflex artery is dominant. In a right dominant circulation, the circumflex artery normally supplies only the lateral and inferolateral walls. The territories of these two arteries can therefore be difficult to distinguish with certainty unless the coronary anatomy is known. It is nearly always safe to assign the anterior wall and septum to the left

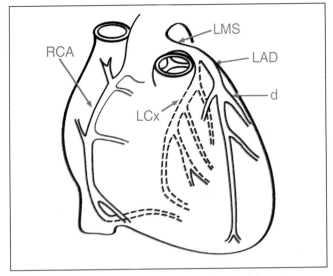

Fig. 1. *Schematic diagram showing the distribution of the major coronary arteries as viewed from the anterior projection. The right coronary artery (RCA) runs between the right ventricle and atrium and usually terminates in the posterior descending artery, which supplies the inferior wall. The left main stem (LMS) quickly divides into 2 main branches. The left anterior descending artery (LAD) descends between the left and right ventricles, supplying the anterior wall, upper septum and usually the apex. It has the diagonal artery (d) as a major branch. The left circumflex artery, (LCx) passes posteriorly between the left ventricle and atrium to supply the lateral wall*

anterior descending artery and the lateral wall to the circumflex artery, but the inferior wall may be supplied either by the right coronary artery or by the left circumflex artery, in accordance with dominance.

Myocardial perfusion imaging is reasonable in defining the number of major vessels involved with coronary artery disease, but because of overlapping arterial territories and varying severity and extent of ischaemia between territories, this is not wholly reliable. It should be noted that there may appear to be an implicit suggestion that myocardial perfusion imaging is in some way less good at assessing prognosis in coronary artery disease because of the difficulty of distinguishing single- and multiple- or three-vessel disease, but this would be quite fallacious. The assessment of prognosis by the number of vessels involved assumes as its basis a prior knowledge of coronary angiography, and it should never be said that myocardial perfusion imaging can demonstrate coronary stenoses. Myocardial perfusion imaging has as its basis a completely different starting point, in demonstrating the summed effect of those stenoses at myocardial level. There is no good reason to try to guess the number of vessels involved with coronary artery disease from the perfusion scan therefore, as this clearly makes a logical error of reasoning. As will be seen in the chapter on assessment of prognosis, the myocardial perfusion study assesses future cardiac risk with a completely distinct method, namely that of the total extent and severity of ischaemia.

COMPARISON WITH THE "GOLD STANDARD" OF ANGIOGRAPHY

Having already said that our understanding of myocardial perfusion imaging has long since transcended banal comparisons of sensitivity with angiography, it is the case historically that angiography has been the gold standard for detection of coronary stenosis. Bearing in mind the limitations and differences between the techniques, the comparison is still used, particularly for the establishment of new tracers and when different forms of pharmacological stress are evaluated in comparison with exercise. The most useful direct comparisons with angiography are probably those which are taken across a broad spectrum of centres, each with varying referral patterns, and this has been achieved with meta-analysis of results in the literature. Such reviews show an overall sensitivity and specificity for the detection of coronary artery disease by perfusion imaging with exercise stress of 84% and 87% (3258 patients) for the planar technique, and 96% and 83% (361 patients) for tomography.[1]

COMPARISON OF DIAGNOSTIC VALUE OF THE VARIOUS STRESS TECHNIQUES

There are now a number of alternative stress techniques to exercise, and it is this in part which has brought perfusion imaging more and more into the clinical arena, because a substantial proportion of patients are unable to exercise to maximal levels for physical or psychological reasons.

The element of inadequate patient capability is removed when pharmacological stress is used, and there have been many comparisons both with exercise perfusion imaging in the same patients and with angiography directly. The most widely used agent currently is dipyridamole and a meta-analysis of 1175 patient studies showed a sensitivity and specificity of 87% and 74% for detection of coronary artery disease.[2] Direct comparison of dipyridamole and exercise studies in 215 patients showed very good agreement.[2] Adenosine thallium imaging has been compared to angiography in 642 patients with a sensitivity and specificity of 87% and 88%.[3]
Direct comparison of adenosine with exercise thallium imaging has also shown very good agreement.[3] Finally, results with dobutamine thallium imaging in five studies in 282 patients to 1993 show sensitivity and specificity of 89% and 96%. These results suggest that a wide range of pharmacological agents may be used to manipulate myocardial perfusion with very similar efficacy to exercise, which considerably lowers the threshold for their clinical use in potentially difficult patients.

SUBMAXIMAL STRESS AND DECREASED SENSITIVITY

There are no surveys of the incidence of so-called athletic incompetence, and estimates would doubtless vary between populations, but perhaps one-third of patients fail to achieve their full exercise potential. Ample evidence in the literature suggests that the results of perfusion imaging with submaximal exercise show a decreased sensitivity for the detection of coronary artery disease.[4,5,6,7] It is therefore unwise to settle for suboptimal stress, as this may result in important disservice to patient management. The assessment of the patient prior to cardiac stress must therefore include an assessment of the patient's exercise potential, preferably coupled with a review of any preceding stress investigations, because the decision to use pharmacological stress is easier when a clinically relevant and recent exercise electrocardiogram has been performed and the exercise performance has been established. A relatively low threshold to the use of pharmacological stress is a reasonable approach, if exercise capability is doubtful.[8]

COMPARISON WITH THE ELECTROCARDIOGRAM IN DIAGNOSIS

It is abundantly clear to busy practitioners of nuclear cardiology that the exercise electrocardiogram can be a very misleading tool. There is a considerable flow of patients to nuclear cardiology who have a low likelihood of coronary artery disease in whom the ST segments become "abnormal" during a routine medical exercise test. A very high proportion of these patients can be shown to have normal myocardial perfusion. Putting arguments aside as to whether the exercise test should have been performed in the first place,[9,10,11] it is quite clear in clinical practice that the false-positive rate of ST segment depression is very high for the detection of coronary artery disease (Table 1). This is borne out in meta-analyses of the diagnostic efficacy of exercise electrocardiography, which show a sensitivity of 81% but a specificity of only 66% in the detection of *multivessel disease* in 12030 patients.[12] A further meta-analysis included 24074 patients with a mean sensitivity of 68% (range 23%-100%) and specificity of 77% (range 17%-100%).[13] The tremendous variability in the findings could not be explained by the known confounding factors such as previous myocardial infarction, digoxin therapy and upsloping ST depression, and suggests that a number of as yet unidentified factors influence the interpretation.

The figures for sensitivity and specificity for myocardial perfusion imaging are apparently superior to those for exercise

84

Abnormal resting electrocardiogram
- Previous myocardial infarction
- Bundle branch block
- Pre-excitation
- Any other cause

Drugs
- Digoxin
- Diuretics (hypokalaemia)
- Anti-arrhythmics

Ventricular hypertrophy
- Systemic hypertension
- Pulmonary hypertension
- Aortic stenosis
- Pulmonary stenosis

Cardiomyopathy
- Hypertrophic
- Dilated

Other
- Smoking/meals prior to exercise
- Females
- Artefact

Table 1 *Causes of ST segment depression during exercise which may not be associated with myocardial ischaemia, causing poor specificity*

electrocardiography (Fig. 2), but comparisons between studies are not scientifically secure, and direct comparisons are much more convincing. One of the best of these used receiver operating characteristic analysis in 771 patients to compare the diagnostic potential of the history, exercise electrocardiogram and thallium scan in determining the presence of coronary artery disease.[14] This showed the statistically significant superiority of thallium imaging (Fig. 3), and the authors concluded "There was a stepwise incremental improvement ... especially from exercise ECG to thallium testing". Studies such

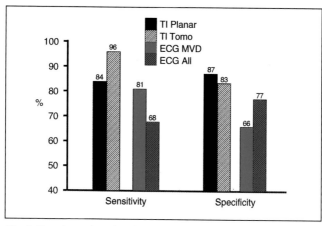

Fig. 2. *Bar chart of results of meta-analysis of relative sensitivity and specificity for thallium imaging and exercise electrocardiography. The comparison suggests superior diagnostic ability of thallium imaging. Tl, thallium; planar, planar imaging;[1] tomo, tomographic imaging;[1] ECG, exercise electrocardiography; MVD, multivessel disease;[12] All, all patients[13]*

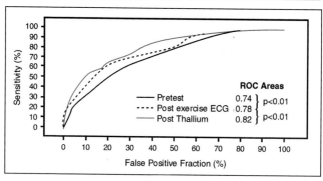

Fig. 3. *Receiver operating characteristic curves derived from a study of incremental diagnostic power of thallium imaging, exercise electrocardiography and the clinical history. There was a significant increase in the area under the curve for the addition of exercise electrocardiography to the history (P<0.01), and for the addition of myocardial perfusion imaging to the combination of exercise electrocardiography with the clinical history (P<0.01). This finding confirms the superiority of thallium imaging in the diagnosis of coronary artery disease compared to exercise electrocardiography. (Reproduced with permission[14])*

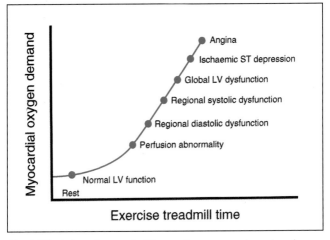

Fig. 4. *The ischaemia cascade. The graph represents the order of physiological events which occur with increasing levels of ischaemia. Perfusion abnormalities occur as a primary event whilst ST segment change and angina occur only much later. This explains the higher sensitivity seen with myocardial perfusion imaging compared with exercise electrocardiography. (Adapted with permission[16])*

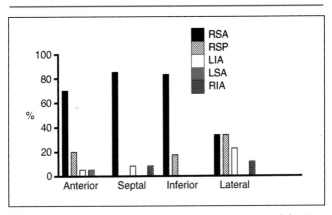

Fig. 5. *Study results showing the poor localisation ability of the ST segment vector on the conventional surface electrocardiogram.[18] Each area of ischaemia is indicated for the four clusters on the horizontal axis. In each case, the most common octant for deviation of the ST vector was the right superior anterior octant, which is equivalent to ST depression in V5. R, right; L, left; S, superior; I, inferior; A, anterior; P, posterior*

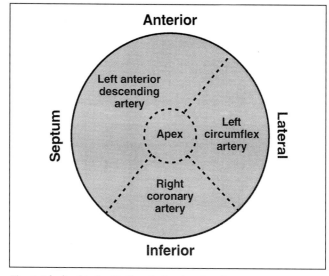

Fig. 6. *Idealised polar (Bullseye) plot showing the commonest distribution of arterial territories. The left anterior descending artery territory is the most reliable. The right coronary territory is correct in 85% of cases, but varies according to arterial dominance of the posterior descending artery. The left circumflex territory can vary considerably in size. The supply to the apex is usually from the left anterior descending artery, but its supply is often mixed, and isolated apical defects may therefore result from disease of any artery*

as these confirm the clinical impression that thallium imaging is a more powerful diagnostic tool than established methods such as exercise electrocardiography, and this is particularly true for patients with limited exercise capability. The superior sensitivity can be explained by reference to the cascade of physiological events which occur with ischaemia (Fig. 4).[15,16]

COMPARISON WITH THE ELECTROCARDIOGRAM IN LOCALISATION

There is a surprising dearth of literature on the capability of the exercise electrocardiogram to localise coronary stenosis, as may be useful for interventional planning. This may relate to the fact that the electrocardiogram appears to be very limited in this regard.[17] The most impressive study comparing thallium imaging with the electrocardiogram for disease localisation showed that the ischaemic ST vector localises to V5 in a majority of cases irrespective of the site of ischaemia, which was clearly depicted by thallium imaging (Fig. 5).[18]

The authors concluded that "Our study demonstrated that ST segment elevation or depression, ..., do not localize ischemia (sic) to myocardial areas or the arteries inferred by these areas". These findings are in direct contrast to the well-established capability of myocardial perfusion imaging to localise ischaemia (Fig. 6).[19]

TYPICAL PATTERNS OF CAD WITH EXAMPLES OF ISCHAEMIA AND INFARCTION

A number of examples of typical patterns of myocardial perfusion abnormality are shown in relation to the clinical situation and the known coronary anatomy. These should serve as a guide to the sort of findings which may be seen in clinical practice. For a fuller series of examples the reader is referred elsewhere.[19]

	VLA	HLA	SA

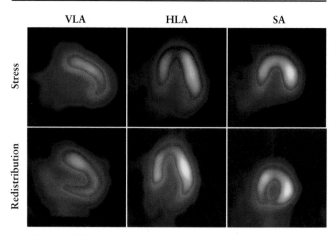

Fig. 7. *Reversible ischaemia with right coronary artery stenosis. There is a defect in the inferior wall in the stress thallium study which shows complete redistribution. (Images reproduced with permission from Thallium myocardial perfusion tomography in clinical cardiology. Pennell, Underwood, Costa, Ell. Springer-Verlag, London 1992)*

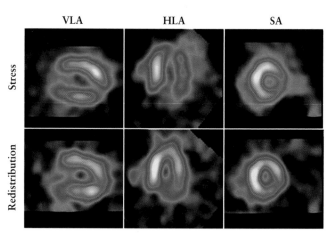

Fig. 8. *Reversible ischaemia with left circumflex artery stenosis. There is a defect in the lateral wall and apex in the stress thallium study which shows complete redistribution*

90

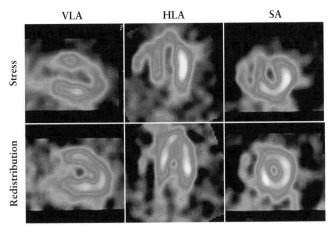

Fig. 9. *Reversible ischaemia with proximal left anterior descending artery stenosis. There is a defect in the anteroseptal wall and apex in the stress thallium study which shows complete redistribution*

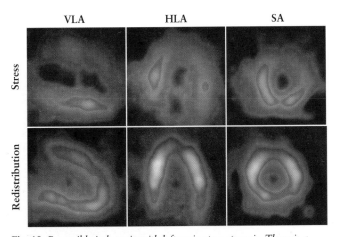

Fig. 10. *Reversible ischaemia with left main stem stenosis. There is a defect in the anterior and lateral walls and apex in the stress thallium study which shows complete redistribution. (Images reproduced with permission from Thallium myocardial perfusion tomography in clinical cardiology. Pennell, Underwood, Costa, Ell. Springer-Verlag, London 1992)*

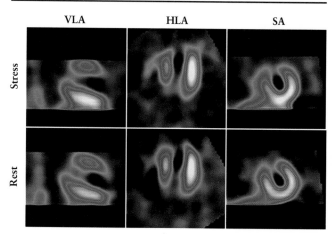

Fig. 11. *Myocardial infarction of left anterior descending artery territory. There is a severe perfusion defect in the stress tetrofosmin images in the anterior wall and apex which extends into the upper septum. There is no significant change with rest imaging suggesting transmural infarction. The left anterior descending artery was occluded*

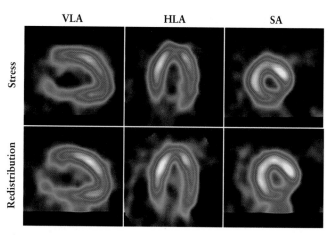

Fig. 12. *Myocardial infarction of right coronary artery territory. There is a severe perfusion defect of the basal and mid inferior wall on the stress thallium images which shows no improvement with redistribution suggesting transmural infarction. The right coronary artery was occluded*

References

1. Kotler TS, Diamond GA. Exercise thallium-201 scintigraphy in the diagnosis and prognosis of coronary artery disease. *Arch Inn Med* 1990; **113**: 684-702.

2. Leppo JA. Dipyridamole-thallium imaging: the lazy man's stress test. *J Nucl Med* 1989; **30**: 281-7.

3. Verani MS. Adenosine stress imaging. *Coronary Artery Disease* 1993; 3: 1145-51.

4. Young DZ, Guiney TE, McKusick KA, Okada RD, Strauss HW, Boucher CA. Unmasking potential myocardial ischemia with dipyridamole thallium imaging in patients with normal submaximal exercise thallium tests. *Am J Noninvas Cardiol* 1987; **1**: 11-14.

5. Heller GV, Ahmed I, Tilkemeier PL, Barbour MM, Garber CE. Influence of exercise intensity on the presence, distribution and size of thallium-201 defects. *Am Heart J* 1992; **123**: 909-16.

6. Iskandrian AS, Heo J, Kong B, Lyons E. Effect of exercise level on the ability of thallium-201 tomographic imaging in detecting coronary artery disease: analysis of 461 patients. *J Am Coll Cardiol* 1989; **14**: 1477-86.

7. Verzijlbergen FJ, Vermeersch PHMJ, Laarman GJ, Ascoop CAPL. Inadequate exercise leads to suboptimal imaging. Thallium-201 myocardial perfusion imaging after dipyridamole combined with low-level exercise unmasks ischemia in symptomatic patients with non-diagnostic thallium-201 scans who exercise submaximally. *J Nucl Med* 1991: **32**: 2071-8.

8. Pennell DJ. Pharmacological cardiac stress: when and how? *Nucl Med Commun* 1994; **15**: 578-85.

9. Diamond GA, Forrester JS. Analysis of probability as an aid in the clinical diagnosis of coronary artery disease. *N Engl J Med* 1979; **300**: 1350-8.

10. McGuire LB. The uses and limits of standard exercise tests. *Arch Intern Med* 1981; **141**: 229-32.

11. Epstein SE. Implications of probability analysis on the strategy used for non-invasive detection of coronary artery disease. *Am J Cardiol* 1980; **46**: 491-9.

12. Detrano R, Gianrossie R, Mulvihill D, et al. Exercise induced ST depression in the diagnosis of multivessel disease: a meta-analysis. *J Am Coll Cardiol* 1989; **14**: 1501-8.

13. Gianrossi R, Detrano R, Mulvihill D, et al. Exercise induced ST depression in the diagnosis of coronary artery disease: a meta-analysis. *Circulation* 1989; **80**: 87-98.

14. Morise AP, Detrano R, Bobbio M, Diamond GA. Development and validation of a logistic reression-derived algorithm for estimating the incremental probability of coronary artery disease before and after exercise testing. *J Am Coll Cardiol* 1992; **20**: 1187-96.

15. Nesto RW, Kowalchuk GJ. The ischemic cascade: temporal sequence of hemodynamic, electrocardiographic and symptomatic expressions of ischemia. *Am J Cardiol* 1987; **57**: 23C-30C.

16. Beller GA. Myocardial perfusion imaging for detection of silent myocardial ischaemia. *Am J Cardiol* 1988; **61(Suppl)**: 22F-26F.

17. Kaplan MA, Harris CN, Aronow WS, Parker DP, Ellestad MH. Inability of the submaximal treadmill stress test to predict the location of coronary disease. *Circulation* 1973. **47**: 250-6.

18. Abouantoun A, Ahnve S, Savvides M, Witztum K, Jensen D, Froelicher V. Can areas of myocardial ischemia be localised by the exercise electrocardiogram? A correlative study with thallium-201 scintigraphy. *Am Heart J* 1984; **108**: 933-41.

19. Pennell DJ, Underwood SR, Costa DC, Ell PJ. Thallium myocardial perfusion tomography in clinical cardiology. London: *Springer,* 1992.

Prognosis in Coronary Artery Disease

INTRODUCTION

There is an enormous literature relating the findings of thallium imaging with the likelihood of future cardiac events, and this has been reviewed in detail.[1] This chapter is a summary which includes more recent work with the ^{99m}Tc agents, and stresses the importance of considering the prognostic findings of a myocardial perfusion study together with the diagnostic findings. The prognostic study of the ^{99m}Tc-based perfusion tracers is less well traced because of their relatively recent introduction and the contemporary problems with studies of the natural history of disease, because of intervention based on extrapolations from the thallium literature.

NORMAL THALLIUM IMAGING

Prognostic value of a normal thallium scan

A large amount of follow-up data is now available on patients who have normal thallium imaging. The important finding has been that there is a very low cardiac event rate (infarction and cardiac death) when perfusion is normal. In Brown's review of the literature to 1991, 3573 patients with normal *planar* thallium imaging from 16 studies with a mean follow-up of 28 months had a cardiac event rate of 0.9% per year,[1] which is similar to that of the general population in the USA.[2] Further data have since become available which include a major study of 3193 patients from France who were studied using thallium *tomography*, and followed for 33 months. This showed that normal SPET images in 715 patients were associated with a cardiac event rate of 0.5% per year.[3]

This apparent improvement may result from the superior definition of areas of abnormality with tomography.

Longer term follow-up in patients with normal planar thallium imaging has also been reported to 10.3 years, with a total cardiac mortality of 1.0%.[4] This again demonstrates a very low predicted event rate and should be compared with the total mortality in the same study of 6.3%, which was mainly cancer related.

The importance of these findings is that when thallium imaging is normal and the scan is technically satisfactory, there is no indication for proceeding to invasive investigations because of the very low cardiac event rate.

Normal thallium imaging in the presence of abnormal exercise electrocardiography

Without dwelling on the poor specificity of exercise electrocardiography, it would be expected that a group of patients would exist in whom the electrocardiogram develops ST segment depression with exercise, despite normal thallium imaging and angiography. The clinical question might arise therefore prior to a decision to proceed to angiography as to whether the electrocardiogram or the thallium scan should be considered the most appropriate for definition of prognosis. This scenario has been directly examined in 164 patients with normal thallium imaging and strongly positive exercise electrocardiography (>2 mm ST depression) with a 34-month follow-up.[5] The cardiac event rate in this group was 0%, strongly suggesting the superiority of the perfusion images for definition of prognosis. Other studies strongly support this finding.[6,7]

ABNORMAL THALLIUM IMAGING

Thallium imaging variables related to prognosis

The variables that have been shown to predict the occurrence of cardiac events using thallium imaging are shown in Table 1.

| Increased lung uptake of thallium |
| Left ventricular dilatation at rest |
| Left ventricular dilatation with stress |
| Extent of perfusion defect |
| Severity of perfusion defect |
| Presence of redistribution |
| Presence of multi-territory abnormality |

Table 1 *Thallium predictors of adverse prognosis in coronary artery disease*

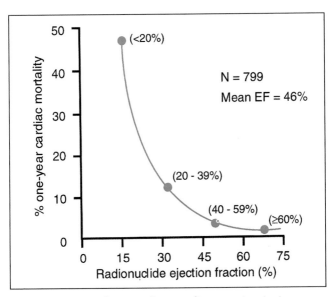

Fig. 1. *One-year cardiac mortality according to resting ejection fraction after myocardial infarction. There is a substantial increase in mortality with decrements in ejection fractions below 40%. Current evidence following the introduction of thrombolytic therapy for infarction suggests that this relationship is still valid. Treatment with other drugs such as angiotensin converting enzyme antagonists may shift the curve to the right. Clearly the ejection fraction is a powerful predictor of prognosis. (Reproduced with permission[8])*

Clinically, the relation between resting ventricular function after infarction and prognosis is well known (Fig. 1),[8] and this is indirectly reflected by ventricular dilatation and lung uptake of thallium. The other important variables directly related to perfusion are the extent and severity of reversible ischaemia.

Lung uptake of thallium Increased lung uptake of thallium is a manifestation of left ventricular dysfunction reflecting high pulmonary capillary pressure at the time of tracer injection.[9] It usually occurs when resting ventricular function is poor, although further superimposed stress-induced ischaemia may co-exist.[9] It is a marker of extensive disease[10,11] and is associated with a poor prognosis. During recovery the thallium clears into the blood as the pressures fall and the timing of acquisition of the heart to lung ratio is critical if quantification is performed.[12] In several studies this variable is the most predictive of an adverse outcome.

Ventricular dilatation Resting ventricular dilatation reflects impaired function, and is an adverse prognostic sign. Ventricular dilation after stress which resolves during redistribution is another marker of extensive coronary artery disease and a poor prognosis.[13] It probably occurs because of extensive subendocardial ischaemia which gives the appearance of a dilated ventricle. The cavity diminishes in size with time because of subendocardial redistribution. There may also be an increase in ventricular diastolic volume following stress. A measurement of dilatation may be made by comparing the cavity area from stress to redistribution (ratio >1.12 indicates a poor prognosis),[13] or the cavity to myocardium counts ratio.[14]

Extent and severity of reversible ischaemia In most patients without prior infarction the prognosis can be determined from the myocardial perfusion scan using the extent and severity of reversible ischaemia. Both of these variables are exponentially related to the risk of future cardiac events, as was elegantly demonstrated by Ladenheim et al. using logistic regression analysis (Figs. 2-4).[15] In this study of 1689 patients with

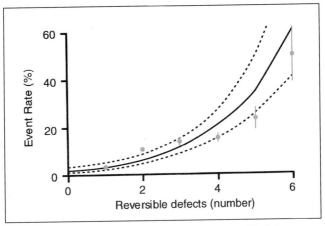

Fig. 2. *The relationship between the* number of reversible defects *found by planar thallium imaging (six-segment model) and the 1-year cardiac event rate. There is an exponential relationship, which clearly demonstrates two important results: that small defects are associated with very little increased risk compared to normal, and that defect size is a major prognostic predictor. (Reproduced with permission[15])*

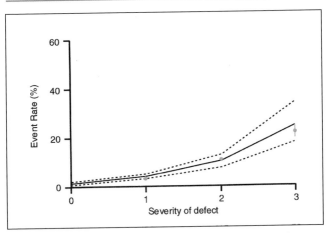

Fig. 3. *The relationship between the* defect severity *found by planar thallium imaging (severity graded from 0 to 3), and the 1-year cardiac event rate. Again, there is an exponential relationship but this is of lower magnitude than for extent of abnormality. Again, it should be noted that the mildest defects are associated with very little increased risk compared to normal. (Reproduced with permission[15])*

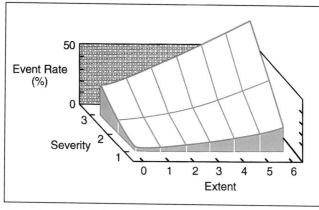

Fig. 4. *Because both the extent and the severity of defects are independent predictors of cardiac events, it is possible to construct a three-dimensional graph of their summed predictive power. This is shown in this figure. The cardiac event rate in this group of patients with low heart rate at peak exercise varied from <1% to 78%. Large and severe defects are associated with a particularly poor prognosis, whilst small and mild defects are associated with little increase in risk. (Reproduced with permission[15])*

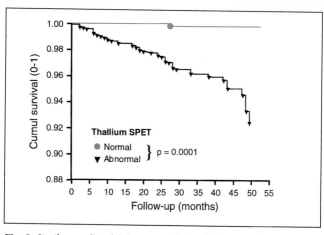

Fig. 5. *Similar results of defect extent being the best predictor of future cardiac events have also been found using tomography. This graph shows the difference in survival between patients with normal or abnormal thallium tomography. The separation of the curves is striking. (Reproduced with permission[3])*

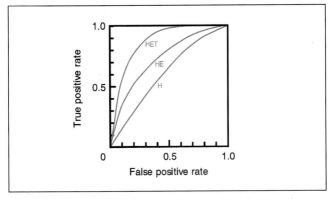

Fig. 6. *Receiver operating characteristic curves for definition of prognosis in a group of patients with abnormal resting electrocardiography. The three curves represent clinical history (H), clinical history plus exercise electrocardiogram (H+E) and clinical history plus electrocardiography plus thallium scintigraphy (H+E+T). Thallium imaging was considerably superior in defining the prognosis compared with exercise electrocardiography (P=0.01). (Reproduced with permission[18])*

suspected coronary artery disease but no previous infarction, the only other clinical variable helpful in discriminating the prognosis was the maximum achieved heart rate with exercise. The cardiac event rate defined from the planar perfusion data ranged from 0.4% to 78% over 1 year. These findings have been confirmed by others.[16] The relation between extent of reversible perfusion defect and prognosis has also been shown for tomography (Fig. 5).[3,17]

These studies show that very small perfusion defects are associated with very little increase in cardiac risk compared with a normal perfusion scan. This emphasises the importance of not over-reporting minor irregularities, as mentioned in the chapter on diagnosis, because the risk from such possible defects is very low, whilst the consequences of false-positive reporting are very adverse.

COMPARISON OF PROGNOSTIC POWER WITH EXERCISE ELECTROCARDIOGRAPHY

Direct comparisons of the prognostic power of exercise electrocardiography and thallium imaging strongly favour scintigraphy. This has been demonstrated using receiver operating characteristic analysis (Fig. 6),[18] and proportional hazards regression models.[17,19] The improved prognostic power of thallium imaging is probably related in part to the improved evaluation of the ischaemic burden, and this without the confounding problems of poor specificity.

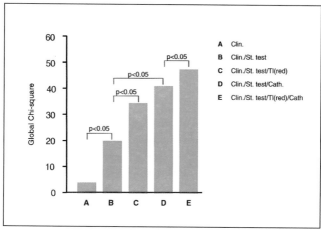

Fig. 7. *The incremental prognostic power of standard cardiac investigations in patients with suspected coronary artery disease. The vertical scale represents prognostic power as the global chi-square value obtained from the regression analysis for the contribution from each variable to the predictive accuracy of the model. There was a significant increment in prognostic power for the addition of exercise electrocardiography to the clinical findings. Alone, planar thallium imaging and coronary angiography added further significant incremental information, and no difference was found in the prognostic power of these two groups. The addition of thallium imaging to all three previous tests significantly added further prognostic information. CLIN, clinical history and examination; ST, test-exercise electrocardiography; TL(red), planar thallium imaging; CATH, coronary angiography. (Reproduced with permission[19])*

COMPARISON OF PROGNOSTIC POWER WITH CORONARY ANGIOGRAPHY

Direct comparisons of the prognostic power of thallium imaging and coronary angiography suggest near equivalence, or superiority of thallium imaging (Figs. 7, 8).[19,17,20,21] Once again this makes a powerful argument for performing perfusion imaging before angiography if patient symptoms are reasonably controlled by medical therapy.

COMPARISON OF PROGNOSTIC POWER AFTER MYOCARDIAL INFARCTION

Before the use of thrombolysis, it was shown that exercise myocardial perfusion imaging was superior to both exercise electrocardiography and coronary angiography in the

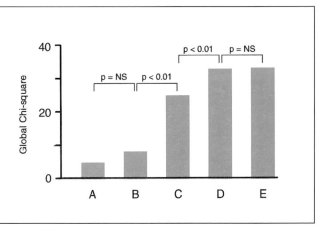

Fig. 8. *Similar analysis to Fig. 7 for tomographic thallium imaging. Bar A shows the prognostic power of gender. The additional information added for each bar is as follows: B + exercise duration, C + exercise duration and coronary angiography, D + exercise duration and thallium tomography, E + all variables. There is a large increment in prognostic power with the use of coronary angiography (C), but thallium tomography alone was significantly superior (P<0.01). In this study, the combination of thallium imaging and coronary angiography showed no incremental prognostic value over the acquisition of the thallium images alone. (Reproduced with permission[17])*

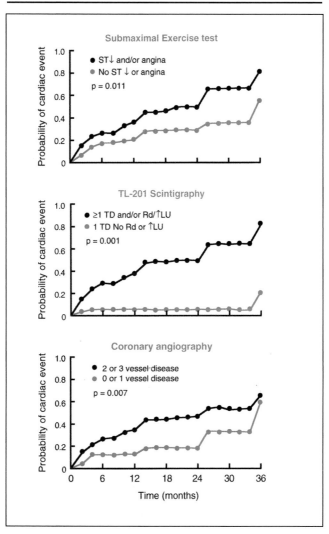

Fig. 9. *Comparison of prognostic power of a pre-discharge
submaximal exercise test, thallium imaging and coronary angiography
in the prediction of future cardiac events after uncomplicated acute
myocardial infarction. The separation of the curves for thallium
imaging (TD=transient defect, Rd=redistribution, Lu=lung uptake) is
statistically superior when compared with the other two techniques
(vs exercise electrocardiography P=0.01, vs coronary angiography
P=0.05). (Reproduced with permission[22])*

definition of prognosis after acute myocardial infarction (Fig. 9).[22] Studies early after infarction have also been performed using dipyridamole and the presence of redistribution was highly predictive of further events, and this was significantly more sensitive than exercise electrocardiography.[23]

Now, in the era of thrombolysis, it has become extremely difficult to repeat such studies,[24] because the results of investigations such as perfusion imaging are being used routinely in risk stratification after infarction such that studies of natural history are restricted to very low risk subgroups, in whom no test (including angiography) may satisfactorily discriminate those patients likely to have a cardiac event because the overall event rate is extremely low.[25,26] The excellent outcomes in patients treated with thrombolysis provide good empirical evidence for the continued use of non-invasive testing along the lines previously defined.

CAN MYOCARDIAL PERFUSION IMAGING PREDICT THE SITE OF FUTURE INFARCTION?

It is now known that infarction occurs as a result of plaque fissuring and the production of thrombus which grows to occlude the coronary artery.[27] The less obvious fact is that in about half of cases, thrombosis causing infarction occurs on stenoses which are not considered significant by conventional criteria.[28,29] Thus although a relationship does exist between stenosis severity and the likelihood of occlusion,[30,31] only in 34% of cases does infarction occur as a result of thrombosis on the site of the most significant stenosis.[32] Presumably therefore, the minor plaques outnumber the more severe stenoses and occlude more frequently on a statistical basis.

Studies of the relationship between the location of a thallium defect and the site of a subsequent infarction also show disparity in 37%-55% of cases,[33,34] but it is important to remember that this does not nullify the predictive accuracy of the imaging for the *occurrence* of the infarction. In all cases in one study, the thallium scan was abnormal despite only predicting the actual site of infarction in 63%.[34] Presumably, the greater the perfusion defect the greater the number and extent of coronary lesions, and this is known to reflect the likelihood of infarction,[35] but predicting the actual location of arterial occlusion is difficult.

PROGNOSTIC VALUE OF THALLIUM IMAGING WITH PHARMACOLOGICAL STRESS

The evidence in the literature suggests that perfusion defects induced by either exercise or the pharmacological agents (adenosine, dipyridamole, dobutamine) produce defects of approximately equivalent size and extent. Therefore there is little reason to suppose that the induction of perfusion defects by whatever means would alter their prognostic value as the common denominator is the underlying disease. This is borne out in the many studies with dipyridamole,[36] and the few studies with adenosine[37] and dobutamine.[38] In patients unable to exercise adequately, however, it is clear that pharmacological stress will give a more accurate picture of risk.

^{99M}Tc-PERFUSION AGENTS

Prognostic value of myocardial perfusion imaging with ^{99m}Tc-perfusion agents

There is little in theory to suggest that the techniques described above for the assessment of prognosis should not also apply to the ^{99m}Tc-labelled agents, because the defect size and severity are very equivalent between the various tracers. The main difference is that lung uptake is not predictive in the same way as for thallium.[39] Normal exercise ^{99m}Tc-MIBI scans are associated with a 0.5% cardiac event rate in the first year,[40] whilst abnormal scans show a greatly increased rate which is a significantly superior predictor to exercise electrocardiography in a regression model.[41] The use of dipyridamole with ^{99m}Tc-MIBI in stable angina[42] or after unstable angina and infarction is also a good predictor of future cardiac events.[43]

PROGNOSTIC POWER OF MYOCARDIAL PERFUSION IMAGING – OTHER SITUATIONS

Prior to major surgery

Major non-cardiac surgery presents considerable risks to patients with coronary artery disease, particularly if the ischaemic burden is masked, as can easily occur in vascular surgery, for example, where coronary artery disease is very common,[44] and patients' exercise potential can be severely limited. In these circumstances, assessment of myocardial perfusion with pharmacological stress can be very helpful in determining which patients are at increased risk from peri–operative cardiac complications, which allows invasive cardiac investigation and revascularisation as appropriate, before the non-cardiac surgery.[45] High risk is reflected in the extent and severity of reversible ischaemia. Extensive fixed defects reflect poor ventricular function and are predictive of peri-operative pulmonary oedema. This has been repeatedly demonstrated using dipyridamole,[46,47] and also adenosine[48] and dobutamine.[38] However, it must be borne in mind that the risk in the overall patient population is not high,[49] and the best results are obtained in using pre-operative screening in those patients with some indication from the history or the electrocardiogram that coronary artery disease may be present.[50,51]

Emergency room chest pain

When patients are received into the emergency room with chest pain, there is often considerable diagnostic difficulty in patients with no typical electrocardiographic changes. Patients may then be admitted unnecessarily, which wastes valuable inpatient resources, or be sent home inappropriately. Studies from Canada and the USA have now demonstrated how injection of ^{99m}Tc-MIBI can be used to accurately differentiate patients for safe discharge. ^{99m}Tc-MIBI is injected during chest pain for best accuracy, with imaging performed after stabilization.[52] The cardiac event rate is very different according to whether the images show normal perfusion or a perfusion defect. Multivariate analysis showed that an abnormal perfusion image was the only independent predictor of a cardiac event (event rate with normal or abnormal scan, 1.4% vs 71% P=0.0004).[53]

Myocardial infarction

Using the ^{99m}Tc-labelled perfusion agents, it is possible to study the perfusion changes associated with thrombolysis at the time of infarction, by injecting at rest before thrombolysis with imaging after stabilization, and subsequently imaging again at rest after some days. This information can be used to study myocardial salvage, which is the difference between the perfusion area at risk before thrombolysis and the final infarct size. This shows that the area at risk is significantly higher from anterior compared with inferior infarction (52% vs 18%), and that therefore the absolute amount of salvage is considerably higher in anterior infarction (16% vs 10%), but the proportion of salvage is similar between the territories.[54] In addition it has been shown that angiography consistently overestimates the area at risk of infarction.[55] Alternatively the efficacy of thrombolysis itself may be assessed, that is whether the infarct-related artery is patent. A significant reduction in the myocardial area at risk is approximately 95% predictive of patency of the infarct-related artery.[56]

This technique has also been used to diagnose myocardial infarction in patients with chest pain and non-diagnostic electrocardiograms who had significant areas of myocardium at risk and who would have benefited from thrombolysis but whose electrocardiographic appearances would otherwise have excluded them.[57]

CLINICAL EXAMPLES

There now follows a series of clinical examples to illustrate how myocardial perfusion imaging may be used to determine prognosis in clinical practice.

	VLA	HLA	SA
Stress			
Redistribution			

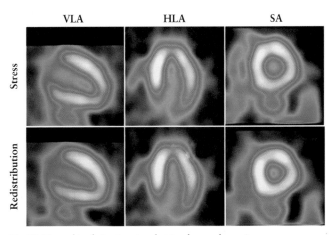

Fig. 10. *Normal perfusion imaging despite abnormal exercise electrocardiography. This study in a female patient with hypertension and very abnormal exercise electrocardiography (4 mm ST segment depression at 6 min of the Bruce protocol) shows normal thallium tomography. The literature shows that perfusion imaging is considerably more powerful as a predictor of future cardiac events than exercise electrocardiography, and that the perfusion scan is more reliable when the results of the two tests are disparate. This relates in part to the poor specificity of exercise electrocardiography in common conditions such as hypertension. This patient had normal coronary arteries*

	VLA	HLA	SA
Stress			
Redistribution			

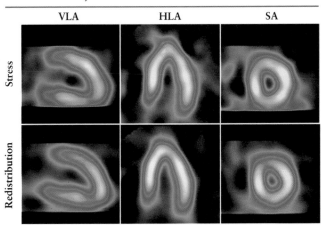

Fig. 11. *Normal perfusion tomography in the presence of coronary artery disease. This patient had moderate coronary artery disease in 2 vessels, with minimal symptoms. The stress and redistribution tetrofosmin images are normal. Despite the known coronary artery disease, the normal perfusion result is very powerful in suggesting a low risk of future cardiac events. Conservative patient management was pursued*

109

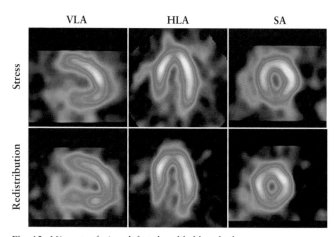

Fig. 12. *Minor perfusion defect, low likelihood of coronary events. Symptoms are a poor guide to prognosis but when the extent and severity of stress thallium abnormality in the basal inferior wall is small, as in this patient, the outlook is good. Invasive investigation was postponed because symptomatic control with medical therapy was possible, and follow-up every 1-2 years with perfusion imaging has not revealed any deterioration*

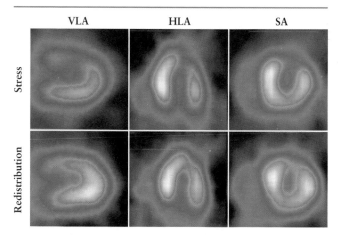

Fig. 13. *Moderate perfusion defect, intermediate likelihood of coronary events. In this case, the thallium abnormality in the mid anterior wall is moderate in size and severity and the patient is at increased risk from cardiac events. Invasive investigation was arranged in this case because of troublesome symptoms, and angioplasty was performed to the diagonal artery*

110

VLA	HLA	SA

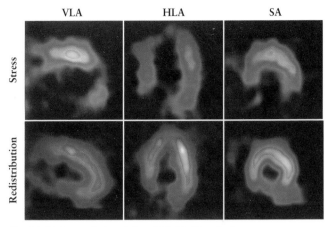

Fig. 14. *Major perfusion defect, high likelihood of coronary events. In this case, there are severe and extensive stress thallium defects throughout the heart, with the exception of the basal and mid anterolateral wall, in addition to inferior myocardial infarction. The extent and severity of the defects indicated a high risk of cardiac events. Invasive investigation was warranted with a view to revascularisation if feasible. In this case, this was pursued and bypass surgery was performed, even though the patient's symptoms were reasonably controlled (images reproduced with permission from Thallium myocardial perfusion tomography in clinical cardiology. Pennell, Underwood, Costa, Ell. Springer-Verlag, London 1992)*

References

1. Brown KA. Prognostic value of thallium-201 myocardial perfusion imaging. A diagnostic tool comes of age. *Circulation* 1991; **83**: 363-81.

2. National Centre for Health Statistics: vital statistics of the United States, 1979: vol II, Mortality, part A. Washington DC, US government printing office, DHHS publication No. (PHS) 84-1101, 1984.

3. Machecourt J, Longere P, Fagret D, et al. Prognostic value of thallium-201 single photon emission computed tomographic myocardial perfusion imaging according to extent of myocardial defect. Study of 1926 patients with follow-up at 33 months. *J Am Coll Cardiol* 1994; **23**: 1096-106.

111

4. Steinberg EH, Koss JH, Lee M, Grunwald AM, Bodenheimer MM. Prognostic significance from 10 year follow-up of a qualitatively normal planar exercise thallium test in suspected coronary artery disease. *Am J Cardiol* 1993; **71:** 1270-3.

5. Schalet BD, Kegel JH, Heo J, Segal BL, Iskandrian AS. Prognostic implications of normal exercise SPECT thallium images in patients with strongly positive exercise electrocardiograms. *Am J Cardiol* 1993; **72:** 1201-3.

6. Wahl JM, Hakki AH, Iskandrian AS. Prognostic implications of normal exercise thallium-201 images. *Arch Intern Med* 1985; **145:** 253-6.

7. Krishnan R. Lu J, Dae MW, Botvinick EH. Does myocardial perfusion scintigraphy demonstrate clinical usefulness in patients with markedly positive exercise tests? An assessment of the method in a high risk subset. *Am Heart J* 1994; **126:** 804-16.

8. The Multicentre Postinfarction Research Group. Risk stratification and survival after myocardial infarction. *N Engl J Med* 1983; **309:** 331-6.

9. Boucher CA, Zir LM, Beller GA, et al. Increased lung uptake of thallium-201 during exercise myocardial imaging: clinical, hemodynamic and angiographic implications in patients with coronary artery disease. *Am J Cardiol* 1980; **46:** 189-96.

10. Lahiri A, O'Hara MJ, Bowles MJ, Crawley JC, Raftery EB. Influence of left ventricular function and severity of coronary artery disease on exercise-induced pulmonary thallium-201 uptake. *Int J Cardiol* 1984; **5:** 475-90.

11. Homma S, Kaul S, Boucher CA. Correlates of lung/heart ratio of thallium-201 in coronary artery disease. *J Nucl Med* 1987; **28:** 1531-5.

12. Mahmood S, Buscombe JR, Ell PJ. The use of thallium-201 lung/heart ratios. *Eur J Nucl Med* 1992; **19:** 807-14.

13. Weiss AT, Berman DS, Lew AS, Nielsen J, Potkin B, Swan HJC, Waxman A, Maddahi J. Transient ischaemic dilatation of the left ventricle on stress thallium-201 scintigraphy: a marker of severe and extensive coronary artery disease. *J Am Coll Cardiol* 1987; **9:** 752-9.

14. Roberti RR, Van Tosh A, Baruchin MA, et al. Left ventricular cavity-to-myocardial count ratio: a new parameter for detecting resting left ventricular dysfunction directly from tomographic thallium perfusion scintigraphy. *J Nucl Med* 1993; **34**: 193-8.

15. Ladenheim ML, Pollock BH, Rozanski A, et al. Extent and severity of myocardial hypoperfusion as predictors of prognosis in patients with suspected coronary artery disease. *J Am Coll Cardiol* 1986; **7**: 464-71.

16. Iskandrian AS, Hakki AH, Kane-Marsch S. Prognostic implications of exercise thallium-201 scintigraphy in patients with suspected or known coronary artery disease. *Am Heart J* 1985; **110**: 135-43.

17. Iskandrian AS, Chae SC, Heo J, Stanberry CD, Waaserleben V, Cave V. Independent and incremental prognostic value of single photon emission computed tomographic (SPECT) thallium imaging in coronary artery disease. *J Am Coll Cardiol* 1993; **22**: 665-70.

18. Ladenheim ML, Kotler TS, Pollock BH, Berman DS, Diamond GA. Incremental prognostic power of clinical history, exercise electrocardiography and myocardial perfusion scintigraphy in suspected coronary artery disease. *Am J Cardiol* 1987 **59**: 270-7.

19. Pollock SG, Abbott RD, Boucher CA, Beller GA, Kaul S. Independent and incremental prognostic value of tests performed in hierarchical order to evaluate patients with suspected coronary artery disease. Validation of models based on these tests. *Circulation* 1992; **85**: 237-48.

20. Kaul S, Lilly DR, Gascho JA, et al. Prognostic utility of the exercise thallium-201 test in ambulatory patients with chest pain: comparison with cardiac catheterization. *Circulation* 1988; **77**: 745-58.

21. Kaul S, Finkelstein DM, Homma S, Leavitt M, Okada RD, Boucher CA. Superiority of quantitative exercise thallium-201 variables in determining long term prognosis in ambulatory patients with chest pain: a comparison with cardiac catheterization. *J Am Coll Cardiol* 1988; **12**: 25-34.

22. Gibson RS, Watson DD, Craddock GB, et al. Prediction of cardiac events after uncomplicated myocardial infarction: a prospective study comparing predischarge exercise thallium-201 scintigraphy and coronary angiography. *Circulation* 1983; **68**: 321-36.

23. Leppo JA, O'Brien J, Rothendler JA, Getchell JD, Lee VW. Dipyridamole-thallium-201 scintigraphy in the prediction of future cardiac events after acute myocardial infarction. *N Engl J Med* 1984; **310**: 1014.

24. Gimple LW, Beller GA. Assessing prognosis after acute myocardial infarction in the thrombolytic era. *J Nucl Cardiol* 1994; **1**: 198-209.

25. Moss AJ, Goldstein RE, Hall WJ, et al. Detection and significance of myocardial ischemia in stable patients after recovery from an acute coronary event. *JAMA* 1993: **269**: 2379-85.

26. Brown KA. Noninvasive risk stratification: right question, wrong study. *J Nucl Cardiol* 1994; **1**: 112-3.

27. Davies MJ, Thomas A. Thrombosis and acute coronary artery lesions in sudden cardiac ischemic death. *N Engl J Med* 1984; **310**: 1137-40.

28. Ambrose JA, Tannenbaum MA, Alexopoulos D, et al. Angiographic progression of coronary artery disease and the development of myocardial infarction. *J Am Coll Cardiol* 1988; **12**: 56-62.

29. Hackett D, Davies HG, Maseri A. Pre-existing coronary stenoses in patients with first myocardial infarction are not necessarily severe. *Eur Heart J* 1988; **9**: 1317-23.

30. Ellis S, Alderman E, Cain K, et al. Prediction of risk of anterior myocardial infarction by lesion severity and measurement method of stenoses in the left anterior descending coronary distribution: a CASS registry study. *J Am Coll Cardiol* 1988; **11**: 908-16.

31. Taeymans Y, Theroux P, Lesperance J, Waters D. Quantitative angiographic morphology of the coronary artery lesions at risk of thrombotic occlusion. *Circulation* 1992; **85**: 78-85.

32. Little WC, Constantinescu M, Applegate RJ, Kutcher MA, Burrows MT, Kahl FR, Santamore WP. Can coronary angiography predict the site of a subsequent myocardial infarction in patients with mild to moderate coronary artery disease? *Circulation* 1988; **78**: 1157-66.

33. Naqvi T, Hachamovitch R, Dev V, Shah PK. Does stress Tc-99m sestamibi/TI-201 myocardial SPECT predict the site of future acute myocardial infarction (abstract)? *Circulation* 1994; **90**: I-102.

34. Jacaruso RB, Steingart RM. Do perfusion defects on stress myocardial perfusion images predict the site of future infarction (abstract)? *Circulation* 1994; **90**: I-23.

35. Moise A, Clement B, Saltiel J. Clinical and angiographic correlates and prognostic significance of the coronary extent score. *Am J Cardiol* 1988; **61**: 1255-9.

36. Hendel RC, Latden JJ, Leppo JA. Prognostic value of dipyridamole thallium scintigraphy for evaluation of ischemic heart disease. *J Am Coll Cardiol* 1990; **15**: 109-16.

37. Kamal AM, Fattah AA, Pancholy S, et al. Prognostic value of adenosine single photon emission computed tomographic thallium imaging in medically treated patients with angiographic evidence of coronary artery disease. *J Nucl Cardiol* 1994; **1**: 254-61.

38. Elliott BM, Robison JH, Zellner JL, Hendrix GH. Dobutamine T1-201 imaging. Assessing cardiac risks associated with vascular surgery. *Circulation* 1991; **84(Suppl III)**: 54-60.

39. Saha M, Farrand TF, Brown KA. Lung uptake of technetium-99m-sestamibi: relation to clinical, exercise, hemodynamic and left ventricular function variables. *J Nucl Cardiol* 1994; **1**: 52-6.

40. Raiker K, Sinusas AJ, Wackers FJ, Zaret BL. One year prognosis of patients with normal planar or single photon emission computed tomographic technetium-99m-labelled sestamibi exercise imaging. *J Nucl Cardiol* 1994; **1**: 449-56.

41. Stratmann HG, Williams GA, Wittry MD, Chaitman BR, Miller DD. Exercise technetium-99m sestamibi tomography for cardiac risk stratification of patients with stable chest pain. *Circulation* 1994; **89**: 615-22.

42. Stratmann HG, Tamesis BR, Younis LT, Wittry MD, Miller DD. Prognostic value of dipyridamole technetium-99m sestamibi myocardial tomography in patients with stable chest pain who are unable to exercise. *Am J Cardiol* 1994; **73**: 647-52.

43. Miller DD, Stratman HG, Shaw L, et al. Dipyridamole technetium-99m sestamibi myocardial tomography as an independent predictor of cardiac event free survival after acute ischemic events. *J Nucl Cardiol* 1994; **1**: 172-82.

44. Hertzer NR, Beven EG, Young JR, et al. Coronary artery disease in peripheral vascular patients; a classification of 1000 coronary angiograms and results of surgical management. *Ann Surg* 1984; **199**: 223-33.

45. Abraham SA, Eagle KA. Preoperative cardiac risk assessment for non-cardiac surgery. *J Nucl Cardiol* 1994; **1**: 389-98.

46. Leppo J, Plaja J, Gionet M, Tumolo J, Paraskos JA, Cutler BS. Noninvasive evaluation of cardiac risk before elective vascular surgery. *J Am Coll Cardiol* 1987; **9**: 269-276.

47. Lette J, Waters D, Lapointe J, Gagnon A, Picard M, Cerino M, Kerouac M. Usefulness of the severity and extent of reversible perfusion defects during thallium dipyridamole imaging for cardiac risk assessment before noncardiac surgery. *Am J Cardiol* 1989; **64**: 276-281.

48. Saw L, Miller DD, Kong BH, et al. Determination of perioperative cardiac risk by adenosine thallium-201 myocardial imaging. *Am Heart J* 1992; **124**: 861-9.

49. Ashton CM, Peterson NJ, Wray NP, Kiete CI, Dunn JK, Wu L, Thomas JM. The incidence of perioperative myocardial infarction in men undergoing non-cardiac surgery. *Ann Intern Med* 1993; **118**: 504-10.

50. Mangano DT, London MJ, Tubau JF, et al. Dipyridamole thallium-201 scintigraphy as a preoperative screening test. A reexamination of its predictive potential. *Circulation* 1991; **84**: 493-502.

51. Baron JF, Mundler O, Bertrand M et al. Dipyridamole thallium scintigraphy and gated radionuclide angiography to assess cardiac risk before abdominal aortic surgery. *N Engl J Med* 1994; **330**: 663-9.

52. Bilodeau L, Theroux P, Gregoire J, Gagnon D, Arsenault A. Technetium-99m sestamibi tomography in patients with spontaneous chest pain: correlations with clinical, electrocardiographic and angiographic findings. *J Am Coll Cardiol* 1991; **18**: 1684-91.

53. Hilton TC, Thompson RC, Williams HJ, Saylors R, Fulmer H, Stowers SA. Technetium-99m sestamibi myocardial perfusion imaging in the emergency room evaluation of chest pain. *J Am Coll Cardiol* 1994; **23**: 1016-22.

54. Christian TF, Gibbons RJ, Gersch BJ. Effect of infarct location on myocardial salvage assessed by technetium-99m isonitrile. *J Am Coll Cardiol* 1991; **17**: 303-8.

55. Huber KC, Bresnahan JF, Bresnahan DR, Pellikka PA, Behrenbreack T, Gibbons RJ. Measurement of myocardium at risk by technetium-99m sestamibi: correlation with coronary angiography. *J Am Coll Cardiol* 1992; **19**: 67-83.

56. Gibson WS, Christian TF, Pellikka PA, Behrenbeck T, Gibbons RJ. Serial tomographic imaging with technetium-99m sestamibi for the assessment of infarct related arterial patency following reperfusion therapy. *J Nucl Med* 1992; **33**: 2080-5.

57. Christian TF, Clements IP, Gibbons RJ. Noninvasive identification of myocardium at risk in patients with acute myocardial infarction and nondiagnostic electrocardiograms with technetium-99m sestamibi. *Circulation* 1991; **83**: 1615-20.

Bypass Surgery

INTRODUCTION

Increasing numbers of coronary artery bypass graft (CABG) operations are being performed, and this is most frequently for angina poorly controlled by medical therapy, or for improvement of prognosis such as in left main stem lesions. Patients usually receive one to five grafts, with at least one internal mammary artery being grafted onto the main vessel such as the LAD, and other vessels receiving venous grafts. Short-term symptomatic relief occurs in approximately 85% of cases, but in time many patients get recurrent symptoms. This is because of progressive occlusion of bypass grafts, and the progression of atheroma in native arteries, which appears to accelerate after grafting.

Before bypass surgery
- A baseline for follow-up studies
- To identify severity and extent of ischaemia for prognosis
- Detection of residual myocardium in areas of infarction
- Detection of hibernating myocardium

After bypass surgery
- Identification of surgical complications
- Documentation of improvement in stress perfusion
- Detection of graft occlusion
- Differentiation of ischaemic from other chest pain
- Detection of disease progression in native vessels

Table 1 *Indications for myocardial perfusion imaging before and after bypass surgery*

MYOCARDIAL PERFUSION IMAGING BEFORE BYPASS SURGERY

Myocardial perfusion imaging may be used to identify functionally significant coronary stenoses, to determine the extent and severity of ischaemic myocardium, to determine the severity of loss of myocardium in areas of infarction, and to detect myocardial hibernation (Table 1). These aspects are covered elsewhere in this book, but American Heart Association and American College of Cardiology guidelines on the indications for bypass surgery include the use of radionuclide techniques to assess the severity of ischaemia.[1]

INDICATIONS FOR POSTOPERATIVE MYOCARDIAL PERFUSION IMAGING

Perfusion imaging can be used to identify peri-operative myocardial infarction, to detect improved perfusion in areas of revascularised myocardium, graft closure and progression of disease in native vessels, and also to differentiate true from non-ischaemic chest pain.

Detection of procedural complications

Coronary artery bypass surgery leads to peri-operative myocardial infarction in 4%-40% of cases.[2] Most commonly new Q waves on the postoperative electrocardiogram and elevation of creatine kinase levels are used to confirm this diagnosis, but creatine kinase levels may be elevated after any surgical intervention and electrocardiographic changes are often non-specific. In such patients alternative methods of diagnosing myocardial infarction are required. Persistent perfusion defects detected for the first time postoperatively indicate peri-operative myocardial infarction.[3]

Documentation of improved perfusion

Perfusion imaging has been used to document improvement in stress myocardial perfusion after CABG,[4] with resolution of pre-operative stress perfusion defects in over 90% of patients.[3]

119

In addition, thallium defects which are present at rest and show redistribution also improve resting thallium uptake after revascularisation.[5] This implies that resting perfusion may also be improved by bypass surgery, and this forms the basis for improved regional wall motion at rest, which is the hallmark of hibernating myocardium. Perfusion imaging has also been used to demonstrate improvements in perfusion and wall motion in patients with unstable angina who have undergone bypass surgery.[6]

Detection of graft occlusion

Early after operation, coronary bypass grafts may become occluded by thrombus, frequently forming at the distal graft-coronary anastomosis. Within the first 2 weeks after bypass surgery, 8%-10% of all venous grafts occlude and by 1 year 12%-16% of venous grafts are occluded. Later, progression of coronary atheroma is the main problem. After 5 and 10 years 20% and 45% of venous grafts are occluded.[7] Furthermore, although other grafts remain patent, significant atheroma often develops such that by 10 years the majority are atheromatous.[8] Internal mammary artery grafts have a longer life span, and when inserted into the left anterior descending artery 95% are patent at 10 years.[9]

Cardiac catheterisation can be used to determine graft patency but the minor risk and invasiveness of the procedure prohibit serial studies. Because of non-specific postoperative changes, bundle branch block and the frequent use of digoxin, exercise electrocardiography is also of relatively low value in the detection of graft occlusion, although the exercise duration may be helpful. Perfusion imaging, on the other hand, is an effective, non-invasive and easily repeatable method of detecting graft occlusion.

In a study of 55 patients before and after CABG, serial thallium imaging had an 80% sensitivity and 88% specificity in detecting graft occlusion, which was predicted by reversible ischaemia as well as by new persistent defects.[3] The results were also correlated with chest pain. Where there were new perfusion thallium defects and the patient had typical or atypical angina there was a high probability (83%) of at least one graft being occluded. In the absence of new perfusion defects, only 5% of patients with no chest pain and 9% with atypical chest pain had an occluded graft. In addition, 61% of occluded grafts were correctly localised by thallium scintigraphy. Where grafts supply small areas of myocardium or previously scarred myocardium or where there are multiple grafts to a single vascular territory, perfusion imaging will not detect graft occlusion.[3] Differentiation of ischaemia in the grafted versus non-grafted areas has also proved possible with thallium imaging,[10] and this is relevant because of accelerated atherosclerosis in native vessels after bypass.[11]

Differentiation of ischaemic from non-ischaemic chest pain

After CABG many patients complain of chest pain, but it is often difficult to differentiate on the basis of symptoms alone which patients have true recurrent angina. Other causes of chest pain after bypass grafting include musculoskeletal chest pain after thoracotomy, pain related to resection of the internal mammary artery, postoperative pericarditis, and anxiety. Direct comparisons between exercise electrocardiography and thallium imaging in the detection of recurrent stenosis after bypass surgery strongly favour perfusion imaging because of the non-specific changes that occur in the ECG with surgery and medication. The comparison on one study for sensitivity was ECG 30% vs thallium 65%, and for specificity ECG 40% vs thallium 100%.[12]

Perfusion imaging accurately identifies patients with underlying ischaemia, and determines its location. This, coupled with a knowledge of the pre-operative coronary anatomy and the location of grafts performed, may enable ischaemic postoperative chest pain to be attributed to either graft or native coronary disease. Thus patients with ischaemic chest pain who may benefit from repeat cardiac catheterisation can be differentiated from those with non-ischaemic chest pain.

	VLA	HLA	SA

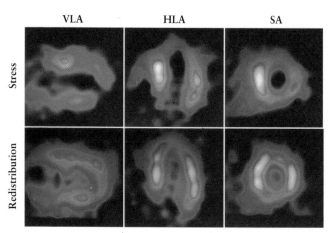

Fig. 1. *Perfusion imaging prior to bypass surgery. A 65-year-old asthmatic man was referred for thallium imaging because of angina 5 years after an inferior myocardial infarction. He had bilateral total hip replacements which limited exercise to 4 min. Perfusion imaging with dobutamine stress showed reversible ischaemia of the anterior wall and apex, and the inferior and lateral walls with infarction of the basal inferior wall. Coronary angiography showed proximal stenosis of all three coronary arteries and inferior hypokinesis and coronary artery bypass grafting was undertaken. Repeat perfusion imaging after bypass is shown in the next case (images reproduced with permission from Thallium myocardial perfusion tomography in clinical cardiology. Pennell, Underwood, Costa, Ell. Springer-Verlag, London 1992)*

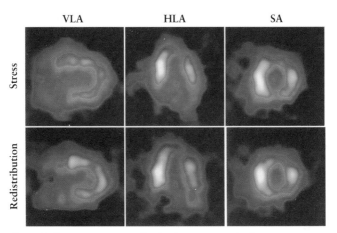

Fig. 2. *Perfusion imaging 6 months after bypass surgery. In the same man as the previous case, the perfusion with stress is now very considerably improved. The basal inferior infarction continues to show no thallium uptake, and the ventricle is less dilated with stress. This study is a useful baseline should symptoms recur (images reproduced with permission from Thallium myocardial perfusion tomography in clinical cardiology. Pennell, Underwood, Costa, Ell. Springer-Verlag, London 1992)*

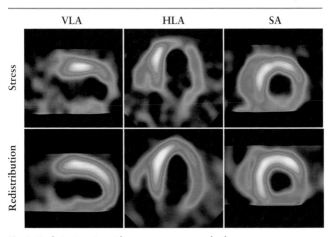

Fig. 3. *Perfusion imaging with recurrent symptoms after bypass surgery. A 50-year-old man was referred for perfusion imaging 6 months after bypass surgery. He had suffered previous myocardial infarction and had persistent postoperative atypical chest pain. Peripheral vascular disease precluded adequate exercise assessment. Stress was performed with adenosine and submaximal exercise. The tetrofosmin images show severe anteroapical and lateral reversible ischaemia with inferior myocardial infarction. Angiography confirmed early occlusion of 2 grafts*

123

References

1. Report of the American College of Cardiology/American Heart Association Task Force on assessment of diagnostic and therapeutic cardiovascular procedures: ACC/AHA guidelines and indications for coronary artery bypass graft surgery. *Circulation* 1991; **83:** 1125-73.

2. Hultgren NH, Shettigar UR, Pfeifer JF, Angell WW. Acute myocardial infarction and ischaemic injury during surgery for coronary artery disease. *Am Heart J* 1977; **94:** 146-53.

3. Pfisterer M, Emmenegger H, Schmitt HE, et al. Accuracy of serial myocardial perfusion scintigraphy with thallium-201 for prediction of graft patency early and late after coronary artery bypass surgery. A controlled prospective study. *Circulation* 1982; **66:** 1017-24.

4. Gibson RS, Watson DD, Taylor GJ, et al. Prospective assessment of regional myocardial perfusion before and after coronary revascularization surgery by quantitative thallium-201 scintigraphy. *J Am Coll Cardiol* 1983; **3:** 804-15.

5. Berger BC, Watson DD, Burwell LR, Crosny IK, Wellons HA, Teates CD, Beller GA. Redistribution of thallium at rest in patients with stable and unstable angina and the effect of coronary artery bypass surgery. *Circulation* 1979; **60:** 1114-25.

6. Kolibash AJ, Goodenow JS, Bush CA, Tetalman MR, Lewis RP. Improvement of myocardial perfusion and left ventricular function after coronary artery bypass grafting in patients with unstable angina. *Circulation* 1979; **59:** 66-74.

7. Fitzgibbon GM, Leach AJ, Kafka HP, Keon WJ. Coronary bypass graft fate: long-term angiographic study. *J Am Coll Cardiol* 1991; **17:** 1075-80.

8. Campeau L, Enjalbert M, Lesperance J, Vaislic C, Grondin CM, Bourassa MG. Atherosclerosis and late closure of aortocoronary saphenous vein grafts: sequential angiographic studies at 2 weeks, 1 year, 5 to 7 years and 10 to 12 years after surgery. *Circulation* 1984; **70(Suppl II):** 1-7.

9. Loop FD, Lytle BW, Cosgrove DM, et al. Influence of the internal mammary artery graft on 10 year survival and other cardiac events. *N Engl J Med* 1986; **314**: 1-6.

10. Ritchie JL, Narahara KA, Trobaugh GB, Williams DL, Hamilton GW. Thallium-201 myocardial imaging before and after coronary revascularisation. *Circulation* 1977; **56**: 830-6.

11. Cashin WL, Sanmarco ME, Nessim SA, Blankenhorn DH. Accelerated progression of atherosclerosis in coronary vessels with minimal lesions that are bypassed. *N Engl J Med* 1984; **311**: 824-8.

12. Iskandrian AS, Haaz W, Segal RL, Kane SA. Exercise thallium-201 scintigraphy in evaluating aortocoronary bypass surgery. *Chest* 1982; **80**: 11-5.

Angioplasty

INTRODUCTION

Percutaneous transluminal angioplasty is an effective method of coronary revascularisation. Initially performed primarily in patients with single-vessel coronary disease, it is now used in multivessel disease, bypass graft stenoses and total coronary artery occlusions. An essential element of any intervention is to assess its effect, and this can be performed using myocardial perfusion imaging to visualise abnormal flow in relation to the known coronary anatomy. It can therefore confirm successful angioplasty, detect and assess complications such as myocardial infarction, and evaluate recurrent symptoms (Table 1).

It is important to point out at this early stage that disturbance of coronary anatomy and endothelial function may be poorly assessed by coronary angiography after angioplasty, and there are frequent discrepant results between angiography and perfusion imaging because of this. The information from the perfusion scan must be interpreted with this knowledge in mind, and used in the overall clinical assessment of the patient.

JUSTIFICATION FOR ANGIOPLASTY

The American Heart Association with the American College of Cardiology has published guidelines for the appropriate use of angioplasty.[1] This discourages the performance of interventional procedures unless symptoms can be related to the findings at coronary angiography,[2] such that patients are only exposed to a procedural risk when symptomatic benefit is likely. The recommendations require that ischaemia be documented before angioplasty either by exercise

Before angioplasty
- Justification for the procedure, in demonstrating myocardial ischaemia localised to the territory appropriate to the proposed artery for dilatation
- Baseline study to allow comparison with all further follow-up studies
- Assessment of culprit lesion

After angioplasty
- Confirmation of improved stress perfusion post angioplasty
- Detection of procedural complications such as infarction
- Early scan – prediction of restenosis before angiographic appearance
- Late scan – detection of restenosis (superior to exercise electrocardiography)
- Assessment of need for further culprit lesion angioplasty

Table 1 *Uses of myocardial perfusion imaging before and after angioplasty*

electrocardiography or radionuclide testing. It can be maintained that it is preferable to perform this by perfusion imaging rather than by exercise electrocardiography because of the superior sensitivity and specificity, as well as greatly superior ability to localise the defect to the territory of coronary stenosis. Whilst these recommendations are not a world-wide policy statement, they nevertheless indicate good practice in ensuring potential patient benefit from a serious procedure, and in addition signal the need for a consistent and coherent baseline functional investigation for follow-up studies in the significant numbers of patients who will require further investigation for recurrent symptoms and restenosis.

DOCUMENTATION OF EARLY IMPROVEMENT IN MYOCARDIAL PERFUSION

Thallium myocardial perfusion imaging documents improvement in regional myocardial perfusion after angioplasty. In one study with documented perfusion abnormalities in 93% of patients before angioplasty, improvement was seen in 76% of patients 1–2 days after angioplasty.[3] Although myocardial perfusion improves after successful angioplasty, residual defects are frequently seen early after successful angiographic dilatation, and there is a relatively poor early agreement between angiography and perfusion imaging for complete revascularisation.

For example, in a study of 43 patients undergoing angioplasty for single-vessel coronary disease, perfusion imaging was performed before, and at mean times afterwards of 9 ±5 days, 3.3 ±0.6 months and 6.6 ±1.2 months.[4] Coronary angiography at 6-9 months documented coronary patency in all patients. Myocardial perfusion in the distribution of the dilated coronary artery was shown to improve progressively until 3 months, but thereafter no improvement was seen.

These findings of slow improvement after successful dilatation have also been found with other techniques. Using intracoronary Doppler assessment of coronary flow reserve in a study of 31 patients, flow velocity was measured immediately after, and at 7.5 months after angioplasty.[5] Immediately after successful angioplasty coronary flow reserve did not correlate with residual stenosis. Only later was a significant relationship seen and in the absence of restenosis, coronary flow reserve was eventually normal in all patients. Using positron emission tomography, there was a similar delay in coronary flow reserve after angioplasty, with recovery over 3 months.[6]

Therefore, whilst improvement in perfusion is the usual finding after successful angioplasty, there is considerable disparity between the function of the coronary resistive vessels and the angiographic appearances. The reasons for this are speculative but might include the prolonged dilatation of the vessels impairing autoregulation, the release of vasoconstrictor substances from the angioplasty site, or distal embolisation.[6]

Another finding of note which is relevant is that the vessel at the site of angioplasty continues to remodel, and improvements in cross-sectional area occur over several months in a substantial proportion of patients.[7]

Therefore it may be difficult to interpret the findings of myocardial perfusion tomography when residual defects are found early after angioplasty unless a pre-angioplasty study has been performed to form the basis for comparison. It is recommended, therefore, that for the detection of restenosis, perfusion imaging is carried out approximately 2 months after the intervention, depending on the clinical situation.

DETECTION OF COMPLICATIONS

Myocardial perfusion imaging can be used to detect procedural complications such as myocardial infarction and side-branch occlusion which are not always detected angiographically or by monitoring cardiac enzymes. If a previously reversible thallium defect becomes fixed after angioplasty, this suggests that intervention-related infarction has occurred.

ASSESSMENT OF THE CULPRIT LESION

Thallium imaging has a unique role in the evaluation and management of patients with multivessel disease. Angioplasty may be staged in these patients, with the most severe stenosis being dilated first and further vessels being considered if symptoms persist or there is evidence of reversible ischaemia in another territory. Perfusion imaging is an effective method of identifying the lesion which is most functionally significant.[8] Repeat thallium imaging after angioplasty of the culprit lesion may reveal residual ischaemia in the same or another arterial distribution and may be used to guide further attempts at revascularisation. This approach has been followed in a study of 85 patients with multivessel disease to identify the most significant stenosis and the need for a further procedure after this lesion had been dilated.[9] All lesions were technically suitable for angioplasty and the magnitude of the reversible perfusion defect was used to define the target lesion.

Before angioplasty, thallium imaging identified the culprit lesion in 93% of patients. One month later two groups had been identified by repeat imaging; 47 patients without and 38 patients with remote ischaemia. One year later, 17% of the first group and 79% of the second group had undergone further angioplasty for recurrent symptoms.

RESTENOSIS AFTER ANGIOPLASTY

Angioplasty has a high primary success rate and the appearance of the coronary angiogram is improved in 80% of patients. Unfortunately, restenosis after an initially successful procedure remains a problem. Reported rates of restenosis vary because there are many definitions with little standardization of method, timing and rate of late arteriography. Restenosis occurs in up to 50% of patients within the first 6 months,[10] with the majority of recurrences being evident by 3 months.[11]

Restenosis can be detected by the recurrence of symptoms, by non-invasive testing or by coronary arteriography, the last of which is limited by expense and minor risks. Symptoms are an unreliable indicator of restenosis because many patients are asymptomatic despite restenosis, as shown in one study where only 34% of patients with restenosis had chest pain during treadmill exercise.[12] In addition, up to 50% have chest pain in the absence of restenosis.[13] The choice of non-invasive tests includes exercise electrocardiography, which is safe, widely available and inexpensive but of limited value for detecting restenosis. It is unhelpful if the resting electrocardiogram is abnormal, and is otherwise associated with a low sensitivity and specificity of 60% and 69%.[14,15] Others have found sensitivities as low as 25% and 24%.[16,17] Unfortunately, even when the exercise electrocardiogram is abnormal, the difficulty in localising areas of ischaemia means that it is difficult to distinguish restenosis from progression or unmasking of disease in other sites.

Perfusion imaging has a number of advantages, therefore, in detecting restenosis, including differentiation from progression of disease in other arteries. In one study, thallium imaging was 86% sensitive, specific and accurate for the detection of.

130

restenosis and results were similar in single- and multiple-vessel angioplasty and after complete or partial revascularisation. Significant stenoses in arteries which were not dilated were detected with a sensitivity of 91%, a specificity of 84% and an accuracy of 85%. In all, 81% of such stenoses were detected. Importantly, in a later study the same group demonstrated that thallium perfusion imaging was equally sensitive, specific and accurate in detecting restenosis in asymptomatic and symptomatic patients.[18]

PREDICTION OF RESTENOSIS

Myocardial perfusion imaging early after angioplasty may show abnormalities which correlate poorly with the angiographic findings but several investigators have now demonstrated that these patients have a much higher likelihood of progressing to later restenosis. One month after angioplasty, reversible ischaemia was predictive of recurrence of angina in 66% and of restenosis in 74% of patients.[19] In contrast, the exercise electrocardiogram was not predictive of recurrent angina or restenosis.

This predictive value has been shown in larger studies including one of 121 patients.[20] Patients who developed symptoms and an abnormal thallium scan were referred for coronary angiography. Reversible ischaemia in the territory of the dilated artery was seen in 26 (25%) of 104 asymptomatic patients 4-6 weeks after angioplasty, and of these 22 (86%) had clinical and angiographic evidence of restenosis at 6 months, as did 25 (96%) at 1 year. Of patients with eventual restenosis, 87% were predicted by the thallium scan just 4-6 weeks after angioplasty. In contrast, patients with a normal scan at 3 to 6 months, with or without associated symptoms, had a very low likelihood of developing restenosis.

The thallium scan performed earlier than 1 month was not predictive of restenosis, probably because of the acute coronary flow changes produced by dilatation. Several groups have studied very early perfusion imaging after angioplasty but the results are not as good as studies using later imaging, with one study using imaging at 12-24 h identifying just 52% of patients with later restenosis.[21]

IMAGING IN THE ABSENCE OF SYMPTOMS

This is a difficult subject because whilst it is known that restenosis is often clinically silent even in patients who suffered angina prior to angioplasty, it is clear that in these circumstances there is no need to repeat the procedure on symptomatic grounds. The question of whether the prognosis can be improved by abolishing the silent ischaemia remains unanswered, and needs to be addressed in formal clinical trials.

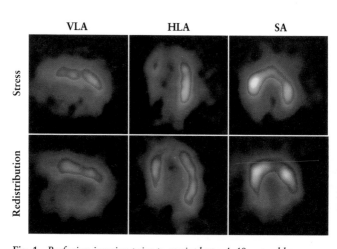

Fig. 1. *Perfusion imaging prior to angioplasty. A 48-year-old man with Wolff-Parkinson-White syndrome was referred for perfusion imaging because of atypical upper chest pain radiating down his left arm. He had previously received steroid injections to his left shoulder for the same complaint. Because of the abnormal resting electrocardiogram, exercise testing was not performed.*
Thallium imaging showed severe inferior reversible ischaemia which extended to involve the apex and inferior septum. Coronary angiography showed a tight proximal right coronary artery stenosis and angioplasty was performed. Repeat perfusion imaging after intervention is shown in the next case (images reproduced with permission from Thallium myocardial perfusion tomography in clinical cardiology. Pennell, Underwood, Costa, Ell. Springer-Verlag, London 1992)

132

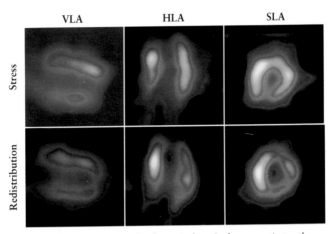

| | VLA | HLA | SLA |

Stress

Redistribution

Fig. 2. *Perfusion imaging 6 months after angioplasty. In the same patient as the previous case, the inferior ischaemia is now abolished. Minor reversible ischaemia is present at the apex. This scan established that revascularisation was successful and is useful for follow-up should symptoms recur (images reproduced with permission from Thallium myocardial perfusion tomography in clinical cardiology. Pennell, Underwood, Costa, Ell. Springer-Verlag, London 1992)*

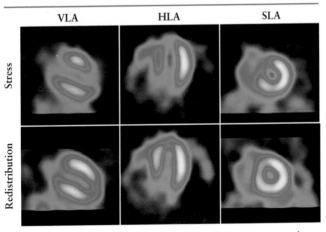

| | VLA | HLA | SLA |

Stress

Redistribution

Fig. 3. *Restenosis with minor symptoms after angioplasty. Four months after angioplasty to the left anterior descending artery, a 50-year-old woman related that she had occasional atypical chest discomfort despite her history of classical angina prior to angioplasty. Perfusion imaging with thallium showed severe ischaemia of the septum and apex, largely sparing the anterior wall. Angiography revealed tight restenosis of the left anterior descending artery sparing a proximal large diagonal branch. Repeat angioplasty was performed despite the minor symptoms*

References

1. Guidelines for percutaneous transluminal coronary angioplasty. ACC/AHA Task Force report. *J Am Coll Cardiol* 1993; **22**: 2033-54.

2. Hilborne LH, Leape LL, Bernstein SJ, et al. The appropriateness of use of percutaneous transluminal coronary angioplasty in New York State. *JAMA* 1993; **269**: 761-5.

3. DePuey EG, Roubin GS, Cloninger KG, King SB, Garcia EV, Robbins WL, Berger HG. Correlation of transluminal coronary angioplasty parameters and quantitative thallium-201 tomography. *J Invasive Cardiol* 1988; **1**: 40-50.

4. Manyari DE, Knudtson M, Kloiber R, Roth D. Sequential thallium-201 myocardial perfusion studies after successful percutaneous transluminal coronary angioplasty: delayed resolution of exercise induced scintigraphic abnormalities. *Circulation* 1988; **77**: 86-95.

5. Wilson RF, Johnson MR, Marcus ML, et al. The effect of coronary angioplasty on coronary flow reserve. *Circulation* 1988; **77**: 873-885.

6. Uren NG, Crake T, Lefroy DC, et al. Delayed recovery of coronary resistive vessel function after coronary angioplasty. *J Am Coll Cardiol* 1993; **21**: 612-21.

7. Johnson MR, Brayden GP, Erickson EE, et al. Changes in cross sectional area of the coronary lumen in the six months after angioplasty: a quantitative analysis of the variable response to percutaneous angioplasty. *Circulation* 1986; **73**: 467-75.

8. Scholl JM, Chaitman BR, David PR, et al. Exercise electrocardiography and myocardial scintigraphy in the serial evaluation of the results of percutaneous transluminal coronary angioplasty. *Circulation* 1982; **66**: 380-390.

9. Breisblatt WM, Barnes JV, Weiland F, Spaccavento LJ. Incomplete revascularisation in multivessel percutaneous transluminal coronary angioplasty: the role for stress thallium-201 imaging. *J Am Coll Cardiol* 1988; **11**: 1183-1190.

10. Nobuyoshi M, Kimura T, Nosaka H, et al. Restenosis after successful percutaneous transluminal coronary angioplasty: serial angiographic follow-up of 229 patients. *J Am Coll Cardiol* 1988; **12**: 616-623.

11. Serruys PW, Luijten HE, Beatt KJ, et al. Incidence of restenosis after successful coronary angioplasty: a time related phenomenon. A quantitative angiographic study in 342 consecutive patients at 1, 2, 3, and 4 months. *Circulation* 1988; **77**: 361-371.

12. Hecht HS, Shaw RE, Bruce TR, Ryan C, Stertzer SG, Myler RK. Usefulness of tomographic thallium-201 imaging for detection of restenosis after percutaneous transluminal coronary angioplasty. *Am J Cardiol* 1990; **66**: 1314-1318.

13. Holmes DR, Vlietstra RE, Smith HC, et al. Restenosis after percutaneous transluminal coronary angioplasty (PTCA): a report from the PTCA registry of the National Heart, Lung and Blood Institute. *Am J Cardiol* 1984; **53**: 77C-81C.

14. Honan MB, Bengtson JR, Pryor DB, et al. Exercise treadmill testing is a poor predictor of anatomic restenosis after angioplasty for acute myocardial infarction. *Circulation* 1989; **80**: 1585-1594.

15. Bengtson JR, Mark DB, Honan MB, et al. Detection of restenosis after elective percutaneous transluminal coronary angioplasty using the exercise treadmill test. *Am J Cardiol* 1990; **65**: 28-34.

16. Laarman G, Luijten HE, Louis GPM, et al. Assessment of "silent" restenosis and long-term follow-up after successful angioplasty in single vessel coronary artery disease: the value of quantitative exercise electrocardiography and quantitative coronary angiography. *J Am Coll Cardiol* 1990; **16**: 578-585.

17. Marie PY, Danchin N, Karcher G, et al. Usefulness of exercise SPECT-thallium to detect asymptomatic restenosis in patients who had angina before coronary angioplasty. *Am Heart J* 1993; **126**: 571-577.

18. Hecht HS, Shaw RE, Chin HL, Ryan C, Sterzer SH, Myler R. Silent ischaemia after coronary angioplasty: evaluation of restenosis and extent of ischaemia in asymptomatic patients by tomographic thallium-201 exercise imaging and comparison with symptomatic patients. *J Am Coll Cardiol* 1991; **17**: 670-677.

135

19. Wijns W, Serruys PW, Reiber JHC, et al. Early detection of restenosis after successful percutaneous transluminal coronary angioplasty by exercise-redistribution thallium scintigraphy. *Am J Cardiol* 1988; **55**: 357-361.

20. Breisblatt WM, Weiland FL, Spaccavento LJ. Stress thallium-201 imaging after coronary angioplasty predicts restenosis and recurrent symptoms. *J Am Coll Cardiol* 1988; **12**: 119-204.

21. Hardoff R, Shefer A, Gips S, et al. Predicting late restenosis after coronary angioplasty by very early (12 to 24 h) thallium-201 scintigraphy: implications with regard to mechanisms of late coronary restenosis. *J Am Coll Cardiol* 1990; **15**: 1486-92.

Hibernation

DEFINITION OF HIBERNATION

It is vital to start a chapter on hibernation with a definition (Table 1), and an understanding of how the term came to exist. "Hibernation" was coined in 1985 by Rahimtoola[1] after some years working in the field of indications for coronary bypass surgery, with particular interest in recoverable ventricular function. He noted that left ventricular function improved in some patients with surgery, and that this phenomenon was seen at least as early as 1971.[2] In 1982, he described a remarkable patient who had single-vessel disease with an occluded left anterior descending artery, and anterior akinesis on the contrast left ventriculogram, with a global ejection fraction of 37%. The appearances were completely compatible with extensive anterior infarction. After the administration of glyceryl trinitrate, however, anterior wall function was seen to improve, and on the basis of this the patient had bypass surgery. Reinvestigation 8 months later showed normal contraction of the anterior wall and an ejection fraction of 76% (Fig. 1).[3] What appeared to be infarcted was not, and full recovery resulted from revascularisation.[4,5]

The definition of hibernation therefore is *clinical*: hibernation exists where important myocardial contraction abnormality shows significant improvement following successful revascularisation. Currently there is no definition other than this, because the basic science of this condition has not yet been fully elucidated. It should be distinguished from other causes of reversible contraction abnormality (Table 2), although only time will tell the exact relationship between hibernation, stunning and silent ischaemia. Notable as well in

Hibernation

- Contractile dysfunction (downgrading) most likely due to reduced resting myocardial perfusion, which at least in the longer term is associated with intracellular loss of contractile protein and glycogen accumulation. It is reversible with revascularisation, but full recovery may take months. At rest, there is no metabolic ischaemia.

Stunning

- Postischaemic contractile dysfunction which persists despite restoration of normal myocardial perfusion in the absence of irreversible damage. An example of the possible clinical circumstances for the occurrence of stunning would include following thrombolysis of an occlusive coronary thrombus.

Silent ischaemia

- Myocardial ischaemia occurring in the absence of angina. Myocardial perfusion is reduced which may result in contractile dysfunction. Recovery is spontaneous when perfusion normalises. Silent ischaemia appears to be relatively common in chronic stable angina.

Viable

- Viable means alive. The term viable can be applied to normal hearts and also those which are myopathic in the absence of coronary artery disease, and cannot therefore necessarily be equated with the need for revascularisation. It is often used to mean hibernation, but it has a completely distinct meaning, and there is considerable potential for confusion with its use. Other terms are more specific and preferable.

Table 1 *Definition of terms commonly used in hibernation literature*

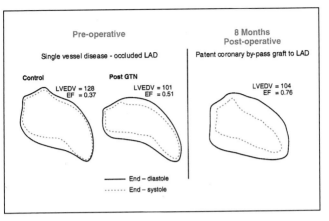

Fig. 1. *The first published case of myocardial hibernation.*
The preoperative findings of anterior and apical akinesia showed some
improvement with glyceryl trinitrate, and bypass surgery was
performed. Eight months after surgery there was normal anterior and
apical contraction. (Reproduced with permission[3])

	Hibernation	Stunning	Silent ischaemia
Contractile function	Decreased	Decreased	Decreased
Reversibility	Revascularisation	Spontaneous	Spontaneous
Myocardial perfusion	Decreased	Normal	Decreased
^{18}F-FDG uptake	Increased	Normal/ increased	Increased

Table 2 *Causes of reversible contraction abnormality in the absence*
of angina

139

this definition, is its retrospective nature. There are only techniques for predicting the presence of hibernation, none of which are definitive. The gold standard in any decent study of hibernation must therefore be contraction before and after revascularisation; all other comparators are surrogates.

CLINICAL OCCURRENCE

Hibernation is not apparently common, but there are no estimates as to its prevalence, and therefore what follows is mainly conjecture. One senior author suggests that the clinical requirement for hibernation studies occurs in 10%-20% of patients referred for coronary angiography,[6] and this is gleaned from an estimate of the numbers with severe ventricular dysfunction, in whom neither severe dilatation nor cardiomyopathy is present. These figures must depend heavily on the referral practice, however. For example, hibernation may be more common after recent rather than old infarction, because coronary occlusion may result in collateral dependent myocardium with poor perfusion, which is the perfect paradigm for hibernation, and it is likely that with time progressive loss of myocardial cells continues. By contrast, another way of looking at hibernation is simply to determine the frequency of improvement in ejection fraction with bypass surgery. This can be as high as one-third of patients[7] (Fig. 2). but unfortunately behind such data is a wealth of changing variables which also affect the ejection fraction, not the least of which is changes in drug therapy, and these results must be interpreted with care.

CLINICAL IMPORTANCE

Fortunately, the clinical importance of hibernation is very much clearer.[8] It is well known that resting ventricular function is closely related to prognosis,[9] and therefore improvement of poor function for patients would be expected to bring significant prognostic benefits. Data to support this already exist from surgical studies where patients with impaired ventricular function can be shown to do very well with revascularisation.[10,11] It is tempting to suggest that such

140

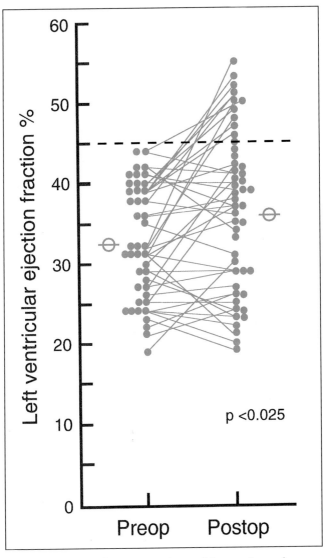

Fig. 2. *One means of gaining an estimate of the prevalence of hibernation is to look at improvements in ventricular function with surgery. In this example, one-third of patients show improvement in ejection fraction, and in some of the cases the improvement is very considerable. Differences in medication and other factors make a complete interpretation difficult. (Reproduced with permission[7])*

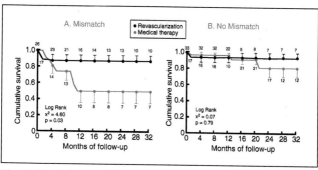

Fig. 4. *Survival curves for patients with hibernation (mismatch) and those without hibernation (no mismatch) according to the use of surgery or medical therapy. In patients with hibernation, surgery significantly improved survival, but in patients without hibernation there was no significant difference between the surgical and medical groups. (Reproduced with permission[8])*

GOOD REASONS NOT TO USE THE WORD "VIABILITY"

The reader may have noticed the conspicuous absence of the term "viability' in this discussion and elsewhere in this book, and this deserves brief explanation. The reason is that the whole area of recoverable contractile dysfunction is littered with confusion over the differences between hibernation and viability. This occurs because "viability" has a number of meanings, some of which have nothing to do with the concept of recoverable contractile dysfunction as envisaged by Rahimtoola. In short, the two concepts are not interchangeable. For example, consider normal myocardium, and also an area of mild partial infarction after thrombolysis, where the feeding artery has a minor 30% residual stenosis. In both cases the myocardial area is viable, but in neither case does the description "viable" help clinically. However, in both cases hibernation is absent, and this *is* helpful as it is clear that revascularisation would not be helpful.

The bottom line is that we wish to apply nuclear cardiology clinically, and to do this we should evaluate ways of accurately assessing hibernation; " viability" is a term which has the potential to confuse and is superfluous to the range of descriptive words we have available.

142

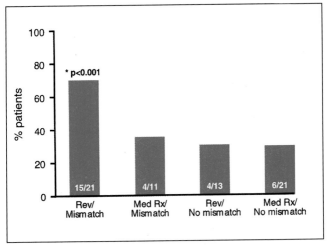

Fig. 3. *Improvement in heart failure symptoms occurs more frequently in patients with hibernation treated by revascularisation than in those with hibernation treated by medical therapy or those without hibernation receiving surgery or medical therapy. REV, revascularisation; Med RX, medical therapy; MISMATCH, hibernation; NOMISMATCH, no hibernation; scar only. (Reproduced with permission[8])*

improvements occur because of revascularisation of hibernating myocardium, although there is no direct evidence for this. However, in small studies of patients with hibernation it has been shown that revascularisation improves symptoms[12,13] (Fig. 3) and prognosis (Fig. 4).[12,13] Another group in whom it is very important not to miss hibernation are patients on the cardiac transplant list. Rahimtoola has suggested that some 10% of these patients have significant hibernation and may improve sufficiently with revascularisation as to not require transplantation.

It is important to remember, however, that the surgical risk in patients with poor function is high and it is not appropriate to suggest that all such patients undergo operation. The clinical requirement is to pick out those patients with significant hibernation who would benefit and in whom, therefore, the risk can be justified. In patients with irreversibly impaired ventricular dysfunction, the risk of surgery and lack of expected benefit are prohibitive.

IS RESTING PERFUSION REDUCED IN HIBERNATION?

Rahimtoola has always envisaged hibernation clinically as representing myocardium with decreased resting perfusion which results in reduced contraction. The matching of perfusion to contraction in the short term is well described,[14] although this has not been shown in the longer term. The clinical evidence for reduced resting perfusion comes from nuclear cardiology studies. Perfusion is decreased to areas of myocardium with increased ^{18}F–fluorodeoxyglucose (FDG) uptake, which are typically found in hibernation.[15] In addition, rest-redistribution of ^{201}Tl is common in areas of hibernation, and this implies that resting perfusion is inappropriately low for the muscle mass present.[16,17,18]

Others disagree with the concept of reduced resting perfusion, however, and suggest that hibernation is actually the result of repetitive episodes of myocardial stunning.[19] Stunning is a quite distinct concept from hibernation and is well characterised in the laboratory. Stunning occurs after an episode of severe ischaemia, which results in delayed recovery of contraction after restoration of perfusion. There is acute contraction-perfusion mismatch, but importantly recovery is spontaneous.[20] It is quite conceivable to envisage a situation where resting myocardial perfusion is relatively normal but quite unable to respond to increases in myocardial oxygen demand such that any exertion leads to ischaemia and stunning (Fig. 5). Evidence for this has been presented by studying collateral dependent myocardium and comparing such areas with and without wall motion abnormality (the former proved to be hibernating segments). In the hibernating segments, resting blood flow was only slightly reduced, and the degree of reduction correlated very poorly with the severity of contraction abnormality. By contrast, in the same areas the perfusion flow reserve, measured using dipyridamole, was well correlated to the degree of contraction abnormality such that the severest contractile dysfunction was seen in patients with exhausted perfusion reserve (Fig. 6).[19]

Further elucidation of this controversy may well rely on development of appropriate animal models, and it is entirely possible that reduced perfusion and repetitive stunning may coexist in hibernation.[15]

144

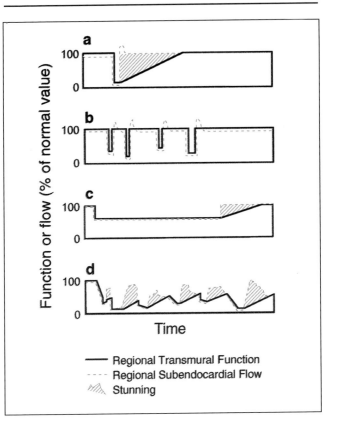

Fig. 5. *Schematic diagrams to illustrate the temporal association between myocardial perfusion and contraction in hibernation, stunning and ischaemia.* Diagram a *illustrates stunning, where a short period of severe ischaemia is followed by a prolonged period of perfusion-contraction mismatch, which recovers spontaneously.* Diagram b *illustrates episodes of ischaemia, which may be silent, in which perfusion-contraction matching occurs without stunning.* Diagram c *shows a possible model of hibernation, where moderately reduced resting perfusion causes prolonged perfusion-contraction matching. Improved perfusion (with revascularisation) may cause immediate recovery if the hibernation is short term, or delayed recovery in the longer term.* Diagram d *shows a possible "real life" scenario, where myocardial perfusion is reduced at rest with perfusion-contraction matching and superimposed on this are episodes of stunning caused by acute and severe ischaemia that might occur with exercise. Such repetitive stunning may explain hibernation, but this is controversial. (Adapted with permission[20])*

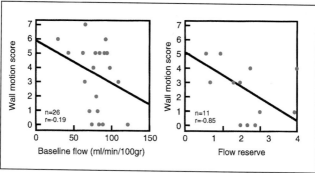

Fig. 6. *Evidence for the repetitive stunning theory of hibernation. The left graph shows the relation between resting perfusion and the wall motion abnormality observed in hibernating segments. A poor correlation is seen and this does not support the notion of perfusion-contraction matching. The graph on the right shows a much better correlation for dipyridamole perfusion reserve with wall motion in the same segments. This supports the notion that stunning might be responsible for the contractile dysfunction.*
(Reproduced with permission[19])

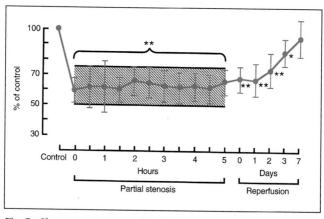

Fig. 7. *Short-term canine model of hibernation produced by reducing resting myocardial perfusion to the subendocardium to 43% of normal. When maintained for 5 h, perfusion-contraction matching was observed, with full recovery of contraction 7 days after restoration of normal perfusion. * P<0.05, ** P<0.01.*
(Reproduced with permission[21])

146

MODELS OF HIBERNATION

There are few animal models for hibernation and none have been stable in the long term. This has considerably hindered a laboratory understanding of chronic hibernation. Matsuzaki demonstrated short-term hibernation, with a controlled reduction of coronary blood flow for 5 h; recovery of contraction was complete after 7 days (Fig. 7).[21] Other short-term models now exist.[22] The most durable model describes reversible contractile dysfunction after coronary flow reduction for up to 7 days.[23] It is noticeable from these studies that reduced perfusion is used to induce the hibernation, but also that the models are rather unstable and loss of animals is not uncommon. Further research in this area will undoubtedly contribute to clinical understanding of hibernation.

IS HIBERNATING MYOCARDIUM ISCHAEMIC?

Classically, ischaemia represents an imbalance between oxygen delivery and demand. If perfusion falls and the myocardium responds by reduced contraction, matching is re-established between supply and demand. It is in the same way that, on restoration of normal perfusion, the myocardium increases its contraction. In this sense therefore the myocardium is not ischaemic at rest, although ischaemia might develop with exercise. The matching of energy expenditure to oxygen supply can be seen as a protective response. In animal models this is borne out by the rapid resolution of lactate production within 2 h following a persistent reduction in myocardial blood supply.[24]

HIBERNATION: HISTOLOGY

Histological comparison between hibernating myocardium, normal areas and infarction has been made using biopsies performed at bypass surgery of the affected territories defined by pre-operative positron emission tomography.[25]
In hibernating myocardium this shows accumulation of intracytosolic glycogen and loss of contractile proteins.

147

There is no increase in fibrosis. The appearances are therefore compatible with an intermediate state between normal myocardium and infarction. The loss of contractile protein suggests that wall motion may be unable to respond to stimulation, and may recover only slowly with restoration of blood flow. The loss of contractile protein has been likened to cellular de-differentiation.

DETECTION OF HIBERNATION USING POSITRON EMISSION TOMOGRAPHY

Hibernation imaging depends on demonstrating its unique characteristics (Table 3). For the purposes of this chapter, the use of positron emission tomography will be summarised briefly. Blood flow is usually assessed using ^{13}N-ammonia or ^{15}O-water. The regional flow is then compared to the regional uptake of a metabolic tracer, namely ^{18}F-FDG. ^{18}F-FDG is trapped in cells which metabolise glucose as a source of energy. Normal myocardial cells preferentially utilise fatty acids, but hibernating myocardium switches to glucose uptake. Hence ^{18}F-FDG uptake in normal myocardium is low compared to hibernating myocardium, which is the opposite pattern from the blood flow. The difference between normal and hibernating myocardium can be very striking (Fig. 8). This technique is outstandingly good in the detection of hibernation because of its metabolic imaging,[26,27] but suffers from expense and limited availability, as well as competition from very good alternatives which are cheaper and widely available. The American Heart Association has recommended that hibernation studies should be performed first with single photon emission tomography, with further study by positron emission tomography only in cases of doubt.[28]

- Significant left ventricular dysfunction at rest

- Prolonged reduction in resting myocardial perfusion
  (see text re. repetitive stunning)

- Perfusion contraction matching (contraction
  downgrading)

- No metabolic evidence of ischaemia (creatine
  phosphate, lactate)

- Metabolically active (^{18}F-FDG uptake increased relative
  to perfusion)

- Reduction in contractile proteins when chronic

- Recruitable inotropic reserve (causes metabolic ischaemia)

- Recovery of contractile function after revascularisation

- Recovery may be delayed for months after revascularisation

Table 3 *Characteristics of hibernating myocardium*

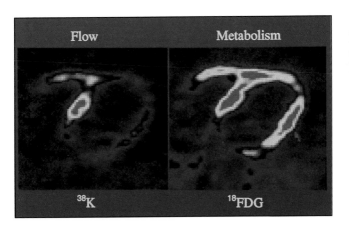

Fig. 8. *Positron emission tomography of hibernating myocardium.
There is reduced perfusion in the lateral wall, which in contrast shows high
regional ^{18}F-FDG uptake. The switch from metabolism of fatty acids to
glucose in the circumstances of reduced perfusion is highly suggestive of
hibernation. (Reproduced with permission from Professor Rigo)*

149

CONVENTIONAL NUCLEAR CARDIOLOGY APPROACHES FOR DETECTION OF HIBERNATION

In conventional nuclear cardiology, the approach to detection of hibernation depends on demonstrating a mismatch between contractile function and the myocardial mass in the same segments. This requires that two issues are accurately investigated: where are the segments with severe contractile dysfunction, and what is the maximum tracer uptake in these areas under ideal conditions? It is usual for the contractile dysfunction to be determined by high-resolution anatomical techniques such as echocardiography, or magnetic resonance imaging. Tomographic techniques are preferred to planar imaging with x-ray contrast ventriculography, which may inadequately survey the entire myocardium. However, more recently, wall motion and wall thickening have been assessed using low-resolution nuclear cardiology techniques with gated tomography of ^{99m}Tc-labelled perfusion agents.[29] The maximal tracer uptake in these segments, which reflects muscle mass, may then be investigated with tomographic perfusion imaging.

The extensive literature on how best to assess perfusion tracer uptake in the areas of abnormal contraction suggests that this is very problematical, but the difficulties lie mainly in the methodological approach rather than the interpretation of the images. Most work has been performed with ^{201}Tl, and problems occur because most laboratories start with a stress redistribution study. It is now well established that the muscle mass present in segments with stress ischaemia may be underestimated by redistribution imaging at 4 h. This is because redistribution may not occur fast enough in the presence of occluded or severely stenosed arteries.[30] This is common in patients undergoing investigation for hibernation. The reinjection technique was proposed to deal with this problem, and improved uptake of ^{201}Tl was demonstrated with this second injection following redistribution imaging in 30%–40% of segments which were otherwise thought to be fixed.[31] This has also been combined with nitrates after stress to improve resting perfusion.[32] Finally, it has been proposed that a separate-day rest injection of thallium should be given to accurately define muscle mass.[16,17,18]

150

Following thallium injection during stress
- Imaging of stress perfusion
- Imaging after 4 h redistribution from stress
- Imaging immediately after reinjection, following 4 h redistribution from stress
- Imaging hours after reinjection, following 4 h redistribution from stress
- Imaging after reinjection, following 4 h redistribution from stress with nitrates
- Imaging immediately after, reinjection immediately after stress imaging
- Imaging 4 h after, reinjection immediately after stress imaging
- Imaging after late redistribution from stress (24 h)

Following thallium injection at rest
- Imaging of resting perfusion
- Imaging after redistribution from rest
- Imaging after redistribution from rest with nitrates
- Imaging after late redistribution from rest (24 h)

Table 4 *Thallium images obtained from various protocols*

In comparing the several techniques, it is useful to consider which images give methodologically "pure" information (Table 4). Stress and rest perfusion is obtained with injection during stress and rest respectively. The best muscle mass image is obtained after the fullest redistribution of a resting injection.[16,17,18] The images obtained after redistribution from stress and the reinjection images are far less "pure" to interpret because of limitations caused by the difficulties in achieving a good representation of muscle mass when the initial image shows such high contrast between segments with high and low uptake. A not dissimilar problem has been shown for use of ^{99m}Tc-MIBI and a 1-day protocol starting with the stress injection.[33] Therefore in theory, a resting injection with redistribution is the best protocol for determining resting perfusion and segmental muscle mass.

In practice this is usually combined with a stress redistribution study on a separate day to examine for additional stress-induced ischaemia. However, it should be noted that this practice is not at all uniform in the nuclear cardiology community, and proponents of the reinjection technique would suggest that it is preferable because of the high concordance with the rest–redistribution technique,[34] and the avoidance of a separate–day study.

In the interpretation of the images, the next issue is comparison of the contraction data with the ^{201}Tl findings. In an ideal situation, when there is segmental hibernation with no partial infarction, the segmental contraction will be impaired and the rest-redistribution images will show near–normal uptake. In addition, the rest images will show reduced perfusion to the affected segment which improves with redistribution. These findings are diagnostic of hibernation and certainly positron emission tomography has nothing to add in these circumstances.

The more common clinical situation, however, is for hibernation to be superimposed on partial infarction, and in these circumstances the rest-redistribution images will fail to show normal uptake because of the reduced muscle mass in the affected segment. The diagnosis of hibernation then depends on finding significant residual muscle mass (Table 5). Once again, resting redistribution may also be demonstrable. The clinical issue which is not yet completely resolved is: How much residual muscle mass is significant? This simply reflects the question of how much muscle must be present after partial infarction to make revascularisation worthwhile. For example, if 90% of myocardium is infarcted in a segment, worthwhile contractile function will never be returned with revascularisation. The problem comes in choosing a suitable clinical threshold for thallium activity. Experience has suggested that when thallium activity reflects a residual muscle mass of less than 50% of normal, then useful contractile function is unlikely to be restored.[18,35,36] This is because the endocardial fibres are the most important in determining ventricular contraction, but are also the first to be destroyed by infarction, which proceeds from the endocardium towards the epicardium.

Imaging
- Stress thallium imaging
- 4 h stress-redistribution imaging
- Rest thallium injection on separate day
- 4 h rest-redistribution imaging

Interpretation
- Accurate description of regional contractile function by:
    - Magnetic resonance imaging
    - Echocardiography
    - Tomographic ^{99m}Tc-labelled perfusion tracer Imaging
    - X-ray contrast left ventriculography
- Comparison of thallium uptake in rest imaging *in areas of significant dysfunction*
- A threshold of 50% of normal uptake is currently considered adequate muscle mass for useful contractile recovery
- Examine for rest redistribution (quantification if necessary)

Other techniques
- Further experience with ^{99m}Tc-labelled tracers required
- Positron emission tomography useful in cases of difficulty

Table 5 *Recommendations for assessment of hibernating myocardium*

^{99m}TC-LABELLED PERFUSION AGENTS AND HIBERNATION

Controversy continues to reign over the use of ^{99m}Tc-labelled perfusion agents in the assessment of hibernation, because of the issue of reduced resting perfusion. In theory, the low perfusion would result in low ^{99m}Tc-labelled perfusion agent uptake in a rest study, relative to the amount of muscle mass present.[37] Unlike ^{201}Tl, which can redistribute over time to overcome this problem, the ^{99m}Tc-labelled perfusion agents are fixed, and underestimation of residual muscle mass might result. This has been the experience of most investigators who have compared the two types of tracer in hibernating patients,[38,39,40] although some centres have found the ^{99m}Tc-labelled tracers to be equally effective.[41] Further careful research is required in this area.

IMPROVEMENT IN EJECTION FRACTION AFTER REVASCULARISATION

Regional contraction in areas of hibernation improves with revascularisation, but this may not in itself increase the ejection fraction. There are few data on the amount of hibernating myocardium in which function must be improved for there to be an increase in the ejection fraction after surgery, but one study showed that 8 or more segments of the ventricle (on a 15-segment analysis) are needed (Fig. 9).[18] However, as noted above, with so many changes in patient drug therapy and other factors that occur with surgery, it is uncertain how reliable this estimation might be. There are likewise few data relating the improvement in patient symptoms to the extent of hibernating myocardium, but experience suggests that symptoms may improve with improved function of rather less myocardium.

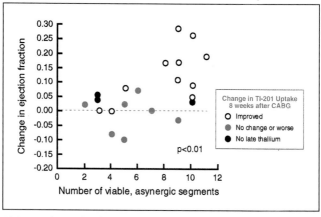

Fig. 9. *Relationship between the number of hibernating segments and the change in ejection fraction following bypass surgery. Significant increases were predominantly seen when eight or more segments of hibernation were identified (this study used a 15-segment myocardial analysis). This also correlated well with improvement in post operative thallium uptake. (Reproduced with permission[18])*

TIME COURSE OF RECOVERY OF CONTRACTILE FUNCTION AFTER REVASCULARISATION

The time course of recovery of contraction of hibernating myocardium varies according to different studies. In patients with unstable angina, immediate improvement has been documented in segmental and global ventricular function.[42] This may represent an acute form of hibernation where no cellular loss of contractile protein has occurred, whereas in patients with poor ventricular function after revascularisation, recovery of ventricular function may take months,[43] and contractile protein recovery may explain this.

Therefore, studies of hibernation particularly in patients with poor ventricular function should always include late follow-up assessment of contractile function.

CLINICAL EXAMPLES

There now follows some clinical examples of the use of conventional nuclear cardiology techniques for the assessment of hibernation.

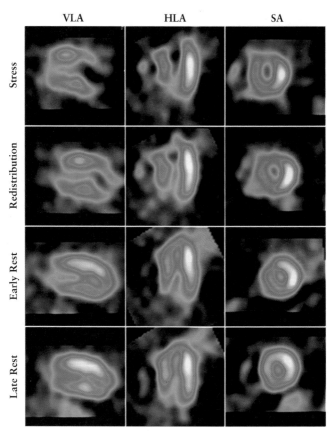

Fig. 10. *Hibernation after anterior myocardial infarction. A 67-year-old man was referred for perfusion imaging 2 months after anterior myocardial infarction. He had undergone quadruple bypass grafting 14 years previously. After the infarction, he had been asymptomatic. Conventional thallium imaging was performed which showed a severe anteroapical defect and moderate inferior and septal defects, and very little redistribution was identified after 4 h. A resting thallium injection was given on a separate day. Considerably improved thallium activity was seen in all the previously abnormal areas and after 4 h redistribution, further improvement was seen in the septum and inferior wall. Akinesis was present in the anterior wall and apex which were considered to be hibernating in view of the high thallium uptake in these areas on the rest study. Extensive ischaemia is present elsewhere. Coronary angiography showed 3 occluded grafts and severe native 3 vessel disease. After surgical revascularisation, the wall motion improved. Thus, despite the infarction, there was considerable residual myocardium in the anterior wall which was reversibly asynergic (hibernating). In addition severe ischaemia was present despite the lack of symptoms*

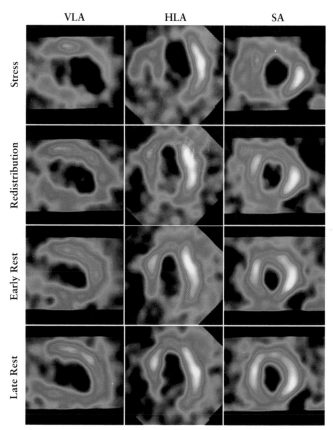

	VLA	HLA	SA
Stress			
Redistribution			
Early Rest			
Late Rest			

Fig. 11. *Hibernation. A 52-year-old man was referred following an episode of pulmonary oedema. Coronary angiography revealed akinesia of the anterior and inferior walls and apex with impaired ventricular function and an ejection fraction of 25%. The right coronary and the left anterior descending arteries were occluded proximally and the left circumflex artery had serial moderate stenosis. Thallium imaging with adenosine and exercise stress showed severe reduction in activity in the anterior and inferior walls, septum and apex. Some improvement was seen with redistribution in the anterior wall and septum. A resting injection of thallium was given on a separate day which showed improvement in uptake throughout the heart, which improved further with redistribution. In view of the known areas of akinesia, hibernation was diagnosed in the anterior and inferior walls and apex. The apparent areas of infarction were therefore considered to be reversibly asynergic and urgent bypass surgery was performed. Considerable improvement in post-operative ventricular function and wall motion was seen on follow up*

References

1. Rahimtoola SH. A perspective on the three large multicentre clinical trials of coronary artery bypass surgery for chronic stable angina. *Circulation* 1985; **72(Suppl V)**: 123-5.

2. Rees G, Bristow JD, Kremkau EL, Green GS, Herr RH, Griswold HE, Starr A. Influence of aortocoronary bypass surgery on left ventricular performance. *N Engl J Med* 1971; **284**: 1116-9.

3. Rahimtoola SH. Coronary bypass surgery for chronic angina – 1981. A perspective. *Circulation* 1982; **65**: 225-41.

4. Rahimtoola SH. The hibernating myocardium. *Am Heart J* 1989; **117**: 211-3.

5. Braunwald E, Rutherford JD. Reversible ischemic left ventricular dysfunction: evidence for "hibernating" myocardium. *J Am Coll Cardiol* 1986; **8**: 1467-70.

6. Iskandrian AS, Heo J, Stanberry C. When is myocardial viability an important issue? *J Nucl Med* 1994; **35(Suppl)**: 4S-7S.

7. Bonow RO, Dilsizian V. Thallium-201 for assessment of myocardial viability. *Semin Nucl Med* 1991; **3**: 230-41.

8. Maddahi J, Schelbert H, Brunken R, DiCarli M. Role of thallium-201 and PET imaging in evaluation of myocardial viability and management of patients with coronary artery disease and LV dysfunction. *J Nucl Med* 1994; **35**: 707-15.

9. The Multicentre Postinfarction Research Group. Risk stratification and survival after myocardial infarction. *N Engl J Med* 1983; **309**: 331-9.

10. Chaitman BR, Fisher LD, Bourassa MG, et al. Effect of coronary artery bypass surgery on survival patterns in subsets of patients with left main coronary artery disease: Report of the Collaborative Study in Coronary Artery Surgery (CASS). *Am J Cardiol* 1981; **48**: 765-77.

11. Passamani E, Davis KB, Gilespie MJ, et al. A randomised trial of coronary artery bypass surgery: survival of patients with low ejection fractions. *N Engl J Med* 1985; **312**: 1665-71.

12. Eitzman D, Al-Aouar Z, Kanter HL, et al. Clinical outcome of patients with advanced coronary artery disease after viability studies with positron emission tomography. *J Am Coll Cardiol* 1992; **20**: 559-65.

13. DiCarli M, Davidson M, Little R, et al. Value of metabolic imaging with positron emission tomography for evaluating prognosis in patients with coronary artery disease and left ventricular dysfunction. *Am J Cardiol* 1994; **74**: 527-33.

14. Ross J. Myocardial perfusion contraction matching. Implications for coronary heart disease and hibernation. *Circulation* 1991; **83**: 1076-83.

15. Conversano A, Herrero P, Geltman EM, Perez JE, Bergman SR, Gropler RJ. Differentiation of stunned from hibernating myocardium by positron emission tomography (abstract). *Circulation* 1992; **86**: I-107.

16. Berger BC, Watson DD, Burwell LR, Crosby IK, Wellons HA, Teates CD, Beller GA. Redistribution of thallium at rest in patients with stable and unstable angina and the effect of coronary artery bypass surgery. *Circulation* 1979; **60**: 1114-25.

17. Mori T, Minamiji K, Kurogane H, Ogawa K, Yoshida Y. Rest injected thallium-201 imaging for assessing viability of severe asynergic regions. *J Nucl Med* 1991; **32**: 1718-24.

18. Ragosta M, Beller GA, Watson DD, Kaul S, Gimple LW. Quantitative planar rest-redistribution Tl-201 imaging in detection of myocardial viability and prediction of improvement in left ventricular function after coronary bypass surgery in patients with severely depressed left ventricular function. *Circulation* 1993; **87**: 1630-41.

19. Vanoverschelde JJ, Wijns W, Depre C, et al. Mechanisms of chronic regional postischemic dysfunction in humans. New insights from the study of non-infarcted collateral dependent myocardium. *Circulation* 1993; **87**: 1513-23.

20. Bolli R. Myocardial "stunning" in man. *Circulation* 1992; **86**: 1671-91.

21. Matsuzaki M, Gallagher KP, Kemper WS, White F, Ross J. Sustained regional dysfunction produced by prolonged coronary stenosis: gradual recovery after reperfusion. *Circulation* 1983; **68**: 170-82.

22. Schulz R, Guth BD, Pieper K, Martin C, Heusch G. Recruitment of an inotropic reserve in moderately ischemic myocardium at the expense of metabolic recovery. A model of short term hibernation. *Circ Res* 1992; **70**: 1282-95.

23. Bolukoglu H, Liedtke AJ, Nellis SH, Eggleston AM, Subramanian R, Renstrom B. An animal model of chronic coronary stenosis resulting in hibernating myocardium. *Am J Physiol* 1992; **263**: H20-9.

24. Fedele FA, Gewirtz H, Capone RJ, Sharaf B, Most AS. Metabolic response to prolonged reduction of myocardial blood flow distal to a severe coronary artery stenosis. *Circulation* 1988; **78**: 729-35.

25. Maes A, Flameng W, Nuyts J, et al. Histological alterations in chronically hypoperfused myocardium. Correlation with PET findings. *Circulation* 1994; **90**: 735-45.

26. Tillisch JH, Brunken R, Marshall R, Schwaiger M, Mandelkorn M, Phelps M, Schelbert H. Reversibility of cardiac wall motion abnormalities predicted by positron tomography. *N Engl J Med* 1986; **314**: 884-8.

27. Tamaki N, Yonekura Y, Yamashita K, et al. Positron emission tomography using fluorine-18 deoxyglucose in evaluation of coronary artery bypass grafting. *Am J Cardiol* 1989; **64**: 860-5.

28. Cardiac positron emission tomography. A report for health professionals from the committee on advances in cardiac imaging and technology of the council on clinical cardiology, American Heart Association. *Circulation* 1991; **84**: 447-54.

29. Chua T, Kiat H, Germano G, et al. Gated technetium-99m sestamibi for simultaneous assessment of stress myocardial perfusion, post-exercise regional ventricular function and myocardial viability-correlation with echocardiography and rest thallium-201 scintigraphy. *J Am Coll Cardiol* 1994; **23**: 1107-14.

30. Gutman J, German DS, Freeman M, et al. Time to completed redistribution of thallium-201 in exercise myocardial scintigraphy: relationship to the degree of coronary artery stenosis. *Am Heart J* 1983; **106**: 989-95.

31. Dilsizian V, Rocco TP, Freedman NMT, Leon MB, Bonow RO. Enhanced detection of ischemic but viable myocardium by the reinjection of thallium after stress-redistribution imaging. *N Engl J Med* 1990; **323**: 141-6.

160

32. He ZX, Darcourt J, Guignier A, Ferrari E, Bussiere F, Baudouy M, Morand P. Nitrates improve detection of ischemic but viable myocardium by thallium-201 reinjection SPECT. *J Nucl Med* 1993; **34**: 1472-7.

33. Taillefer R, Gagnon A, Laflamme L, Gregoire J, Leveille J, Phaneuf D. Same day injections of Tc-99m methoxy isobutyl isonitrile (hexamibi) for myocardial tomographic imaging: comparison between rest-stress and stress-rest injection sequences. *Eur J Nucl Med* 1989; **15**: 113-7.

34. Dilsizian V, Perrone-Filardi P, Arrighi JA, Bacharach SL, Quyyumi AA, Freedman NMT, Bonow RO. Concordance and discordance between stress-redistribution-reinjection and rest-redistribution thallium imaging for assessing viable myocardium. Comparison with metabolic activity by positron emission tomography. *Circulation* 1993; **88**: 941-52.

35. Dilsizian V, Freedman NMT, Bacharach SL, Perrone-Filardi P, Bonow RO. Regional thallium uptake in irreversible defects: magnitude of change in thallium activity after reinjection distinguishes viable from non-viable myocardium. *Circulation* 1992; **85**: 627-34.

36. Bonow RO, Dilsizian V, Cuocolo A, Bacharach SL. Identification of viable myocardium in patients with coronary artery disease and left ventricular dysfunction: comparison of thallium scintigraphy with reinjection and PET imaging with ^{18}F-fluorodeoxyglucose. *Circulation* 1991; **83**: 26-37.

37. Rocco TP, Dilsizian V, Strauss HW, Boucher CA. Technetium-99m isonitrile myocardial uptake at rest. II. Relation to clinical markers of potential viability. *J Am Coll Cardiol* 1989; **14**: 1678-84.

38. Maurea S, Cuocolo A, Pace L, et al. Rest injected thallium-201 redistribution and resting technetium-99m methoxyisobutylisonitrile uptake in coronary artery disease: relation to the severity of coronary artery stenosis. *Eur J Nucl Med* 1993; **20**: 502-10.

39. Cuocolo A, Maurea S, Pace L, et al. Resting technetium-99m methoxyisobutylisonitrile cardiac imaging in chronic coronary artery disease: comparison with rest-redistribution thallium-201 scintigraphy. *Eur J Nucl Med* 1993; **20**: 1186-92.

161

40. Dilsizian V, Arrighi JA, Diodati JG, et al. Myocardial viability in patients with chronic coronary artery disease. Comparison [99mTc]-sestamibi with thallium reinjection and [18F]-fluorodeoxyglucose. *Circulation* 1994; **89**: 578-87.

41. Udelson JE, Coleman PS, Metherall J, et al. Predicting recovery of severe regional ventricular dysfunction. Comparison of resting scintigraphy with [201Tl] and [99mTc]–sestamibi. *Circulation* 1994; **89**: 2552-61.

42. Carlson EB, Cowley MJ, Wolfgang TC, Vetrovic GW. Acute changes in global and regional rest left ventricular function after successful coronary angioplasty: comparative results in stable and unstable angina. *J Am Coll Cardiol* 1989; **13**: 1262-9.

43. Nienaber CA, Brunken RC, Sherman CT, et al. Metabolic and functional recovery of ischemic human myocardium after coronary angioplasty. *J Am Coll Cardiol* 1991; **18**: 966-78.

Radionuclide Ventriculography

INTRODUCTION

Radionuclide ventriculography is an accurate and reproducible way of assessing left ventricular function. The mean inter- and intraobserver variability of assessing ejection fraction is <2%,[1] and the interstudy variability is <5%[1] at rest and <2% with exercise.[2] These excellent results make longitudinal studies of ejection fraction by radionuclide ventriculography very useful. However, the role of radionuclide ventriculography is falling with the development of more reliable echocardiographic techniques, and today approximately only 10% of clinical studies of left ventricular function use radionuclides.

The reasons for this are that many cardiologists are trained in echocardiography, the equipment is portable, enabling studies to be performed at the bedside, and the examination painless and harmless. M-mode echocardiography can be used to measure left ventricular dimensions, and two-dimensional echocardiography can be used to assess global and regional function. When combined with the anatomical detail and the assessment of valves with Doppler, this technique has proved very useful for study of ventricular function.

There are problems with echocardiography, however, the most important of which are that: the quality of echocardiographic assessment of individual patients depends on the skill of the operator, with assessment of ejection fraction by different operators in the same patient varying by 15%;[3] studies are technically very difficult in approximately 10% of patients, such as those with lung disease, and imaging is less than ideal in up to 30%; evaluation of the inferior wall of the left ventricle is difficult; the technique is forced to make assumptions about ventricular geometry for a quantitative assessment of function which yields only semiquantitative results that are considerably worse in badly impaired ventricles; and the result of the inadequate assessment is that the reproducibility of the technique is poor, with an interobserver variability of 11% for ejection fraction.[3] This worsens in badly impaired ventricles.

Recently, automatic boundary edge detection methods have become available, which have improved the assessment of a non-uniform left ventricle, but the methodological flaw of geometric assumptions of shape still remains. This is not a problem suffered by radionuclide ventriculography and it is worthy of note that in major studies of survival and ventricular function with pharmacological treatments such as thrombolysis,[4,5] ß-blockade[6] and angiotensin-converting enzyme inhibition,[7] radionuclide ventriculography was the preferred mode of assessment. Hence, there is still a role for radionuclide ventriculography and where echocardiography is unavailable or experience is limited, radionuclide imaging plays a greater role.

TYPES OF STUDY AVAILABLE

Two types of radionuclide study may be performed. For *first-pass ventriculography* a bolus of tracer is imaged as it passes through the cardiac chambers, and for *equilibrium ventriculography* a tracer that remains in the vascular space is imaged over several hundred beats. Both types of study provide information about global and regional left ventricular function, ventricular volume and diastolic function. Only the first-pass method is capable of identifying and quantifying cardiac shunts. First-pass ventriculography requires either a high count rate gamma camera or a multicrystal gamma camera system. These are unavailable to many nuclear medicine departments and equilibrium radionuclide ventriculography is therefore the more commonly performed study. Most clinical requests are for information about global and regional left ventricular function and currently there is little clinical demand for information about ventricular volumes or filling.

CLINICAL INDICATIONS

The current clinical uses for radionuclide ventriculography in the assessment of left ventricular function are as follows:

Prognosis and treatment after myocardial infarction
Left ventricular ejection fraction is a strong predictor of late outcome after myocardial infarction. The annual mortality in survivors of a first myocardial infarction was 22% in patients with LVEF <30% and 1% in patients with LVEF >30%.[8] An echocardiographic assessment of residual ventricular function may not be sufficiently accurate clinically to indicate risk when the ventricle is badly damaged, and radionuclide ventriculography is relatively more indicated in these patients.[9]

There is also a role for accurate delineation of left ventricular function before starting angiotensin-converting enzyme (ACE) inhibitor treatment after acute myocardial infarction. In the Survival and Ventricular Enlargement (SAVE) study,[10] captopril was given to 2331 patients with asymptomatic left ventricular dysfunction (ejection fractions less than 40% measured by radionuclides). Over 3.5 years, captopril treatment was associated with significant reductions in all-cause (19%) and cardiovascular mortality (21%). A reduction in the incidence of progressive heart failure was primarily responsible for the reduced mortality. The preliminary results of ISIS 4 (International Study of Infarct Survival) showed that captopril given within 24 h of infarction was associated with a small but significant improvement in mortality equivalent to 4.6 lives per 1000 patients. In order that all patients who will benefit from ACE inhibitors are identified, it is desirable that left ventricular ejection fraction is measured after myocardial infarction. Although one study showed similar results with the identification of patients by clinical signs of heart failure,[11] reliance on the clinical appearance may potentially deprive a number of patients from the benefits of ACE inhibition.

Risk stratification before surgery Ventricular function is a strong predictor of operative and postoperative complications. Ventriculography is particularly valuable in patients undergoing peripheral vascular or aortic surgery who represent a higher than average surgical risk due to the frequent coexistence of coronary artery disease. Approximately 40% of deaths during and after major elective vascular surgery are due to cardiovascular events such as myocardial infarction, malignant arrhythmia and heart failure. The lower the ejection fraction the higher the intra-operative and postoperative risk.

Cardiotoxicity Adriamycin is a cancer drug which is associated with a dose-dependent cardiotoxicity. This is rare below a cumulative dose of 350 mg/m^2 but at doses above 550 mg/m^2, approximately one-third of patients develop cardiotoxicity; some patients show severe left ventricular dysfunction with smaller doses because of concomitant cardiac disease, mediastinal radiation or advanced age. Resting radionuclide ventriculography is used before treatment to exclude unsuspected cardiac disease, and for longitudinal follow-up because of its good reproducibility. Patients with a baseline ejection fraction <30% are at high risk for cardiotoxicity and should probably not be started on adriamycin. For patients with a baseline ejection fraction of <50%, repeat ventriculography is recommended when the cumulative adriamycin dose exceeds 300 mg/m^2. High-risk patients given adriamycin require more frequent monitoring. Any patient developing dyspnoea, orthopnoea or ankle oedema during treatment should be restudied. Toxicity is indicated by a fall in absolute ejection fraction between studies of >10%. Further deterioration in left ventricular function may be prevented by a change of chemotherapeutic agent; in some cases existing ventricular damage may improve.

Thalassaemia Patients with thalassaemia may require regular blood transfusions. Over a period of years haemosiderosis may develop with iron deposition within the myocardium. Serial monitoring of left ventricular function identifies those patients with evidence of cardiomyopathy; the benefits of chelation therapy are as yet unproven in this condition.

166

Assessment for cardiac transplantation Although all such patients undergo cardiac catheterisation and coronary angiography, contrast ventriculography is often omitted because of the fluid load and left ventricular ejection fraction can be assessed using radionuclide ventriculography.

Detection of left ventricular aneurysms Using functional images left ventricular aneurysms are easily detected; the function of unaffected left ventricular regions can be established and the effects of aneurysmectomy on ventricular function predicted.

Cardiac shunts Several methods of measuring left to right shunts using radionuclides have been described and these are well validated. Doppler echocardiography is also used but the technique is operator dependent and usually regarded as being semiquantitative.

Uncommon indications Although it is possible to diagnose coronary artery disease using radionuclide ventriculography, exercise electrocardiography and thallium myocardial perfusion imaging are more appropriate first-line investigations. Radionuclide ventriculography is sometimes used to assess the severity of valvular regurgitation, and this can be achieved by examining the stroke volume ratio, which is the ratio of left to right ventricular stroke volume (mean 1.4, normal range 1.1-1.7). The value is usually above unity because of underestimation of the right-sided stroke volume. This simple parameter is raised in left-sided and reduced in right-sided regurgitation. Combined left- and right-sided regurgitation may cause normalisation of the ratio, however.

EQUILIBRIUM RADIONUCLIDE VENTRICULOGRAPHY

Radiopharmaceuticals

Equilibrium radionuclide ventriculography is commonly performed with ^{99m}Tc pertechnetate-labelled autologous red blood cells, although ^{99m}Tc human serum albumin can be used. Serial imaging can be performed for up to 12 h after labelling. The current maximum dose permitted is 800 MBq, and dosimetry to the patient is low (effective dose equivalent 7 mSv, 0.0085 mSv/MBq).

Labelling

There are three methods of labelling red blood cells, all of which use the same principles. When ^{99m}Tc is added to blood it passively diffuses into red blood cells and reducing agents prevent ^{99m}Tc diffusion back out of the red blood cells, by causing tight binding to the beta chain of haemoglobin.[12]

The *in vivo* technique is the quickest and easiest, but results in the lowest labelling efficiency and target to background ratio. The *in vitro* method gives the highest labelling efficiency and target to background ratio but is technically more difficult. The *modified in vivo* technique is intermediate with respect to both these factors.

Stannous ion is used as the reducing agent.[13] The dose is approximately 10-20 µg stannous ion per kg body weight, and it is injected intravenously as a bolus. While exact dosage is not critical, too little tin will not reduce all of the ^{99m}Tc pertechnetate in the red blood cells and this results in free ^{99m}Tc pertechnetate and high background levels. With too much tin, some of the ^{99m}Tc will be reduced before it enters the red blood cells.

In vivo method Stannous ion, normally obtained from a suitable commercial kit (such as Amerscan Stannous Agent from Amersham International) is injected intravenously followed by ^{99m}Tc pertechnetate after approximately 20 min.

Digoxin	Reduces red cell labelling rate
Propranolol	Increases dissociation between red cell and ^{99m}Tc
Heparin	Oxidises stannous ion
Dextrose	Complexes with ^{99m}Tc
Penicillin	Induces red cell antibodies

Table 1 *Common drugs which interfere with red cell labelling*

Imaging commences after a few minutes to allow adequate mixing of tracer and blood. A labelling efficiency of 85%-95% is achieved. A number of drugs and solutions interfere with red blood cell labelling and some of these are shown in Table 1.

In vitro technique This has a labelling efficiency that approaches 100%. A sample of blood is taken, and the red cells are separated and incubated first with stannous ion and then with ^{99m}Tc pertechnetate. The cells are washed with saline before and after each step to eliminate unbound material. The cells are reinjected into the patient with little or no free pertechnetate. The disadvantages of this technique are the handling of blood through multiple steps and the duration of the labelling process, which takes approximately 30 min.

Modified in vivo technique This is easier to perform than the *in vitro* method and results in a lower background than the *in vivo* method. A labelling efficiency of 90%-95% is achieved. The red cells are treated with stannous ion *in vivo* and after 15-30 min a 5-10 ml blood sample is withdrawn into a syringe containing the anticoagulant acid citrate dextrose solution and the ^{99m}Tc pertechnetate dose. The syringe is agitated for 10 min before the labelled blood is reinjected.

Data acquisition

The patient is positioned supine on the imaging couch with the left arm above the head and the electrocardiogram (ECG) leads are attached in standard positions. Because data are

Electrocardiographic gating
Frame mode
16 frames (systolic function study), 32 frames (diastolic function study)
20% window at 140 keV
64 x 64 matrix
Low-energy general-purpose collimator
Left anterior oblique view for best septal separation, with 10-15° caudal tilt (additional left posterior oblique view if possible for inferior wall)
5000 kcounts per view

Table 2 *Typical acquisition parameters for rest radionuclide ventriculography*

acquired using gating to the R wave of the patient's ECG, a good signal is required. Typical acquisition parameters for rest radionuclide ventriculography are shown in Table 2. Prior to starting data acquisition the heart rate is sampled for 10-20 s and the mean RR interval for sinus rhythm determined. Any beats greater than 10% longer or shorter than the mean RR interval are rejected. The patient should be at rest during the sampling period and subsequent data acquisition to avoid major shifts in heart rate. If the heart rate changes substantially during imaging, the beat histogram should be reviewed and the mean RR interval reset. The window for acceptable beats should not exceed 30% of the mean RR interval if meaningful data are to be acquired.

Fluctuations in heart rate can lower the counts and distort the last few frames of the time-activity curve. For further processing where the form of the time-activity curve is important, such as in diastolic function analysis, frames with too low counts should be disregarded, or a correction should be made for this fall off.

Frame mode acquisition The R wave identifies the start of each cardiac cycle. The period between each R wave is divided into a number of intervals or frames, and the counts occurring in the same frame of each cycle are summed into a single image. At least 16 frames per cardiac cycle are required to calculate an ejection fraction. Studies may be acquired for a fixed number of beats or for total counts in the complete study. Fixed count studies usually require 4-6 million counts for the entire study. Fixed beat studies usually acquire for 200-800 individual beats and the time of acquisition depends on heart rate. Approximately 200-350 kcounts per frame are required to obtain an adequate signal to noise ratio.

To prevent patient movement each acquisition should be completed as rapidly as possible.

List mode acquisition List mode data acquisition may also be used. During acquisition the x-y coordinates of each scintillation event are stored separately in computer memory, along with the ECG gating signal and timing markers. When acquisition is completed, a histogram of the cardiac cycle lengths can be generated and a suitable RR interval for the study selected. Acceptable beats will be used to generate images which can be framed in the most appropriate timing interval for the type of analysis required. List mode allows flexible processing of data but requires a large amount of computer memory and additional processing time.

Other dysrhythmia rejection techniques Several methods have been designed to selectively reduce or eliminate irregular beats. The first is postbeat filtration. As the computer acquires each cardiac cycle it checks the RR interval and compares it against predetermined acceptable limits. If the RR interval falls outside these limits no further beats are acquired until the RR interval returns to normal. Unfortunately the initial irregular beat is included in the study. Postbeat filtration deals poorly with frequent isolated irregular beats. The second is dynamic beat filtration. Data from each cardiac cycle are first placed in a temporary storage buffer within the computer rather than being added to the image frames. The computer then checks that the RR interval falls within predetermined acceptable limits. If the beat is not acceptable the data in the temporary buffer are discarded. With this method every irregular beat falling outside the predetermined limits is eliminated.

Camera positioning

Estimation of left ventricular ejection fraction is only possible from the left anterior oblique projection and this view is usually performed first. The heart should be positioned centrally within the field of view. The camera is positioned to obtain the best separation of the left and right ventricles, which is typically around 45°. Caudal tilt of around 10° is applied to the camera. This ensures that an ellipsoid image of the left ventricle is acquired and minimises overlap of the left ventricle by the left atrium. The closer the camera to the patient, the better the spatial resolution of the images. Unfortunately, the application of caudal tilt moves the camera away from the patient. The use of a slant hole collimator with a 15-30° angulation of the holes to the perpendicular obviates the need for tilting of the camera head.

The left anterior oblique projection demonstrates the lateral, infero-apical and septal segments of the heart. It also shows much of the right ventricle. Attenuation of counts from the inferior portion of the blood pool means that the inferior wall is poorly seen in the left anterior projection. This is better seen in the left lateral or 45° left posterior oblique projection. These projections also show the apical and anterior wall segments. The anterior projection, which is less commonly used, shows the anterolateral and apical segments of the left ventricle.

Image processing

The images are scaled to the hottest pixel and displayed in a colour scale to represent the counts in each pixel. Different types of filtering/smoothing are used to improve their appearance and help interpretation. Smoothing can be spatial (within each frame) or temporal (between frames). Spatial filtering corrects each pixel using a weighting algorithm to average counts from surrounding pixels. Temporal smoothing averages pixel information from the preceding and subsequent images to produce a pixel count. Although the smoothed images may be used for display, the original images must be used for background estimation and the generation of ventricular volume curves or significant errors will occur.

Estimation of left ventricular ejection fraction

Identification of the edges of the blood pool at end-diastole and end-systole is performed either manually or using a computer-generated edge detection programme. The first frame of the study is taken as end-diastole and the frame with the lowest left ventricular count as end-systole. Edge detection programmes are most accurate where the target to background ratio is high. In more difficult cases manual definition of the left ventricle is best. Background correction is necessary because some counts within the left ventricle originate from tissue lying in front or behind the heart, and these may account up to 50% of total ventricular counts. It is impossible to measure these counts directly so it is usual to assume that the count density from an area inferolateral to the ventricle is a close approximation to that in front and behind the ventricle. Activity from extracardiac vascular organs such as the liver and spleen should not be included within the background region of interest; this should be 2-3 pixels wide and placed on the end-systolic image.

A time-activity curve for the left ventricle at each frame in the cardiac cycle may then be generated. Calculation of ejection fraction is possible because there is a direct relation between ventricular activity and its volume. Left ventricular ejection fraction (LVEF) is calculated by dividing the background-corrected difference in end-systolic and end–diastolic counts, by the end-diastolic counts.

Estimation of right ventricular ejection fraction

The main problem in estimating right ventricular ejection fraction (RVEF) is that overlap between the right atrium and ventricle occurs. Phase images help to distinguish the right ventricle and atrium but exclusion of pulmonary artery activity remains a problem.

Normal ranges

The normal range for LVEF is between 50% and 70% but each department should establish its own normal values and inter- and intra-observer reproducibility. Ideally, variation between observers and serial studies should be less than 5%. Because stroke volumes are equal on both sides of the heart but the right ventricular end-diastolic volume is larger than the left, right ventricular ejection fraction (RVEF) is lower than LVEF. The normal range for RVEF is 45%-60%. Normal ranges for LVEF and RVEF are similar for children aged 1 year or over.

Accuracy of ejection fraction measurement

The accuracy of ejection fraction measurement is affected by a number of factors, some of which are listed in Table 3. Poor definition of the left ventricular region of interest may occur if there is patient movement, high background activity due to poor red cell labelling, or excess soft tissue attenuation. Because the left atrium fills as the ventricle empties, poor separation or left atrial enlargement may add counts to the left ventricular region of interest at end-systole, causing an underestimation of ejection fraction. Poor separation of the ventricles also leads to an underestimation of LVEF.

Poor gating, attenuating artefacts over the left ventricle and inappropriate background subtraction will also influence the accuracy of ejection fraction calculation. Subtraction of too much background leads to an overestimation of LVEF while

Poor definition of blood pool edges
Poor separation of left and right ventricles
Poor separation of left ventricle and left atrium
Poor gating
Significant soft tissue attenuation over left ventricle
Inappropriate background subtraction

Table 3 *Reasons for poor-quality studies*

subtraction of too little background results in a falsely depressed LVEF. In general, outside the boundary of the region of interest on the background-subtracted end-diastolic image, the counts should fall to zero. However, background subtraction techniques vary between the equipment manufacturers and the most important issue is to ensure a reproducible result. This is to allow longitudinal follow-up of patients.

Image analysis

Endless cine loop display This allows evaluation of the heart throughout the entire cardiac cycle. Regional wall motion can be assessed qualitatively. The left ventricular wall can be divided into segments and a score from 1 to 5 assigned to individual segments depending on whether its motion is normal, hypokinetic (moderate or severe), dyskinetic or akinetic.

Regional ejection fraction Alternatively, it is possible to assess regional ejection fraction quantitatively. Typically this is done by determining the geometric centre of the left ventricle and then dividing this into segments by constructing radii from this. Once the ventricle has been divided, analysis of the count rate during the cardiac cycle can be used to generate regional left ventricular volume curves. Regional ejection fraction can then be determined for multiple segments of the left ventricle.

Functional imaging

In functional images, each pixel is colour coded to represent the value of a particular parameter. They are static images but usually display dynamic parameters. Those most commonly used in cardiac work are the phase and amplitude images. Functional images are generated using Fourier analysis, a mathematical technique which approximates the left ventricular volume curve with the first harmonic Fourier transform, equivalent to a symmetrical cosine curve. The fitted curve can be characterised by its amplitude and the phase angle. Amplitude images therefore show the magnitude of contraction throughout a cardiac cycle and phase images show the timing of peak contraction. The phase angle of a region is expressed in degrees, from 0° to 360° over the RR interval.

Two areas which contract with the same timing appear the same colour in the phase image, while areas with delayed contraction have higher phase values and appear a different colour. It is usual to mask the phase image to show no phase where amplitude is below a certain percentage of maximum, typically 20%. A major limitation of this technique is that an inadequate number of counts can give rise to artefacts.

Phase data may also be represented in histogram format where the number of pixels with a particular phase value is plotted against phase. In normal individuals there are two definite peaks on such a histogram, one representing atrial systole, the other representing ventricular systole. Normally, the left ventricular phase histogram should be a narrow peak representing the simultaneous contraction of all ventricular regions. The standard deviation of phase angle for a region of interest can be calculated; this is a measure of the breadth of the histogram and is normally less than 10-12°. Increased standard deviation of phase occurs when there are regional wall motion abnormalities. Although coronary artery disease is the commonest cause of regional contraction delays, such delays also occur in a variety of conduction disorders.

Normal images A normal amplitude image is characterised by a smaller amplitude in the atria than in the ventricles, and by a greater amplitude in the left than the right ventricle. In the left ventricle it is usual to find the smallest amplitude at the base and the greatest at the apex. Both ventricles should show the same phase although right ventricular amplitude can be quite variable, causing apparent defects even in normal subjects. The atria contract with opposite phase to the ventricles and they appear in a colour corresponding to a very high phase approximately 180° around the cyclical colour scale.

Uses Phase and amplitude images may be used to help define a region of interest when calculating left ventricular ejection fraction. The atria and ventricles can be clearly distinguished; the free borders of the ventricles can also be defined since areas outside the heart have no amplitude. These also help in the identification of regional ventricular contraction abnormalities and aneurysm.[15]

176

Diastolic function analysis

Although systolic abnormalities are responsible for the majority of clinical symptoms in heart failure, abnormal filling of the ventricle or diastolic dysfunction may cause symptoms in some patients. The four phases of diastole (isovolumetric relaxation, rapid early filling, late filling and atrial systole) can be recognised from the radionuclide ventriculogram. In order to derive these more complex parameters, usually a four-function Fourier transform fit is applied to high temporal resolution data with at least 24 frames per cardiac cycle. The type of diastolic information generated consists of peak rates and the time at which these peak rates occur. Conventionally these rates are normalised to the volume or counts present at end-diastole and expressed as end-diastolic volumes/second. Unfortunately heart rate, medication, age and loading conditions can affect diastolic function and caution must be exercised in interpreting abnormalities as indicative of ischaemic heart disease.

STRESS RADIONUCLIDE VENTRICULOGRAPHY

Indications

The assessment of global and regional ventricular function during exercise can be used to diagnose and assess coronary artery disease, but myocardial perfusion imaging is more commonly used because it is methodologically easier and tomographic coverage of the ventricle is more straightforward, which makes it more robust in clinical practice. In the best centres, results with radionuclide ventriculography can be attained which are comparable to myocardial perfusion imaging.

Method

Treadmill exercise causes movement-induced artefacts during stress radionuclide ventriculography, and supine or upright bicycle exercise is preferred. Bicycle ergometers are generally equipped with shoulder restraints and hand grips to minimise movement. Strapping of the chest to the support frame also helps. The blood

177

pressure and ECG are monitored. Imaging is performed in the left anterior oblique projection at rest using the same frame rate and acquisition time that will be used for the exercise study. Typical imaging parameters are shown in Table 4. Exercise is usually started at a workload of 25 W and increased by 25 W every 3-4 min. At each stage, time is allowed for the heart rate to stabilise and data acquisition occurs during the last 2-3 min. The usual end points of the test are significant arrhythmia or hypotension and inability of the patient to continue because of fatigue, dyspnoea or pain. Serial ejection fraction is calculated for rest and each exercise stage. Visual assessment for regional wall motion is performed at each stage. As an alternative to exercise, pharmacological stress may be used and the usual choice is the ß-agonist dobutamine, as described in the chapter on stress methods.

Interpretation

The normal response of the ejection fraction at peak exercise is a rise of ≥ 5 units above the resting value. A drop or a failure to increase with exercise is considered an abnormal response. The reported sensitivity and specificity for coronary artery disease with radionuclide ventriculography are approximately 90% and 85% respectively. However, some patients have an abnormal exercise response in the absence of coronary artery disease. The higher the resting ejection fraction, the smaller the percentage increase during exercise.

Perform resting study using parameters as in Table 2
Perform staged bicycle exercise starting at 25 W, with 3-min increments of 25 W
At each stage of exercise allow 1 min for stabilisation of heart rate
Repeat left anterior oblique acquisition at each exercise level for 2 min

Table 4 *Typical acquisition parameters for stress radionuclide ventriculography*

There is a smaller increase in ejection fraction with increasing age, and the elderly may even show a small decrease. ß-Blockers may blunt the rise in ejection fraction with exercise in normals, and false-positive responses may also occur in non-ischaemic cardiomyopathy, valvular disease and conduction abnormalities such as left bundle branch block.

Ventricular volumes

Volumes may be calculated using a geometric method (involving planimetry and an area-length method) which assumes the left ventricular cavity to be ellipsoid. Unfortunately in patients with deformed left ventricles, geometric assumptions about shape are inappropriate. Counts-based techniques equate counts within the left ventricle to volume, and so make no assumptions about shape, but attenuation of left ventricular counts by surrounding structures is a problem. This has most commonly been tackled by using an attenuation correction for each individual patient. Imaging in the left anterior oblique projection is performed as usual. Before the camera is moved away a point radioactive source is placed on the patient's chest over the centre of the left ventricle. The camera is then rotated to the anterior projection parallel to the patient's chest and a static image acquired. Using trigonometry the distance between the marker on the chest wall and the centre of the left ventricle in the left anterior oblique projection is calculated. A 10 ml blood sample is taken from the opposite arm to that which received the pertechnetate injection, and this is counted at the end of the cardiac study to determine the count rate/ml. This count rate is corrected for radioactive decay between the times of sampling and counting. Attenuation-corrected left ventricular volumes are calculated using $V = V_a(e^{-\mu d})$ where V_a=uncorrected left ventricular volume, μ=linear attenuation coefficient (assumed to be 0.12–0.13) and d=attenuating distance.

Marking the exact centre of the left ventricle is difficult. Even small errors in attenuation distance cause large errors in calculated left ventricular volumes. Nevertheless, ventricular volumes calculated using counts-based methods correlate better with those derived from contrast ventriculography than with geometrically derived radionuclide volumes.

The techniques are not commonly used clinically, because of the similar results that can be obtained with echocardiography, or better with MRI.

Tomography

As with planar imaging, the patient's heart rate is sampled before imaging to define the mean RR interval.

The acquisition of 50 beats which fall within 15% of the mean RR interval is needed before the camera will rotate to the next angle. Each planar acquisition is gated to produce a series of images spanning the cardiac cycle, and the oblique tomographic slices are subsequently reconstructed. If the patient's heart rate is irregular, tomographic imaging may prove either a very lengthy procedure or impossible. Where the heart rate is regular, acquisition time is a little longer than for planar imaging, but processing time is considerably increased. Tomography is not commonly performed because of the extra time and computing capabilities required.

FIRST-PASS RADIONUCLIDE VENTRICULOGRAPHY

A sequence of short duration frames is acquired to show the transit of a bolus through the heart. Cardiac function is assessed from just a few beats and data acquisition can be completed within 60 s. There is a high target to background ratio with temporal separation of the right and left ventricles, but imaging is possible in only one projection.

Radiopharmaceuticals

Many isotopes and ^{99m}Tc-labelled compounds may be used for first-pass imaging because most remain intravascular during the first pass through the central circulation. If the first-pass study is to be followed by an equilibrium study, ^{99m}Tc pertechnetate is used. If serial studies are required, for example at rest and peak exercise, the initial rest study may be performed with an agent such as ^{99m}Tc-DTPA which is cleared rapidly by the kidneys. This allows a repeat injection 20 min later during peak exercise. Dosimetry considerations limit the total number of first-pass studies that may be performed at any one time using ^{99m}Tc agents. Isotopes such as ^{178}Ta, ^{81m}Kr, ^{191m}Ir and ^{195m}Au have also been used for first-pass studies.

Data acquisition

Very high count rates are generated as the entire bolus falls within the field of view. Either a gamma camera with a high count rate capability interfaced to a high-speed computer, or a multicrystal camera is required. Ideally a count rate capability of at least 150 kcounts/s is required to generate an adequate count density for accurate cardiac analysis. Gating is performed and data acquisition should be started just before injection and continued for 10-15 s after passage of the bolus through the heart. Data acquisition is usually performed in list mode. In a typical first-pass study, before background correction, the peak count density in the left and right ventricles will be 1000 counts/frame and 3000 counts/frame respectively.

Camera positioning

Optimal separation of the right atrium and right ventricle is achieved with the right anterior oblique view, but the anterior projection may be superior for assessing both left and right ventricular function. Left ventricular data are attenuated in the left anterior oblique projection, but this is useful for studies totally restricted to the right ventricle. Typical acquisition parameters for first-pass radionuclide ventriculography are shown in Table 5.

Injection technique

The radionuclide bolus should be injected rapidly using a large-gauge cannula in a large vein so the tracer appearance in the right ventricle, lungs and left ventricle is well separated in time. The right arm is preferred because venous return from

181

Electrocardiographic gating
List mode with subsequent conversion usually to 30 ms frames
30% window at 140 keV
64 x 64 matrix
Low-energy, general-purpose collimator
Right anterior oblique view
Frames per cardiac cycle depends on heart rate

Table 5 *Typical acquisition parameters for first-pass radionuclide ventriculography*

this limb has a shorter and less tortuous course to the right atrium and the arm is abducted to straighten the veins.

The radionuclide dose should be in a volume of less than 1 ml, and up to 800 MBq may be injected. The radionuclide bolus is placed into the cannula, which is flushed immediately afterwards with 10 ml of normal saline.

Image processing

Before analysing a first-pass study the quality of the bolus should be checked. A region of interest over the superior vena cava should show a bolus activity curve lasting less than 4 s. If the bolus is unsatisfactory, the study should not be further analysed. As many as 10% of studies are invalid because of a poor injection or problems from concomitant right heart disease, pulmonary hypertension and right ventricular dysfunction.

Estimation of left ventricular ejection fraction

The transit of the bolus can be viewed by continuous dynamic cine display. A good understanding of cardiac anatomy is essential if regions of interest are to be correctly defined. Functional images may assist in distinguishing valve planes.

The ventricle should first be distinguished from the ascending aorta, a region of interest drawn around the left ventricle and a time-activity curve generated. As the bolus remains in the ventricle for several cycles, the time-activity curve shows a series of undulations, the troughs and peaks of which correspond to end-systole and end-diastole. The cardiac cycles containing the maximum activity are then summed in phase, to form a composite curve. The ejection fraction can also be calculated from each of the curves to make an average value from several cycles. Background subtraction is necessary to remove scatter from neighbouring structures such as the left atrium and lungs. Where LVEF is being calculated, background activity can be taken as that in the ventricular region of interest before the arrival of the bolus.

Estimation of right ventricular ejection fraction

In the left anterior oblique projection used for equilibrium radionuclide ventriculography there is significant overlap of the right ventricle by the right atrium and therefore first-pass ventriculography is considered superior for right ventricular ejection fraction evaluation. RVEF is calculated in much the same way as LVEF except that background subtraction is not usually necessary. There are a number of clinical settings in which measurement of RVEF is useful; these include investigation of the patient with unexplained dyspnoea, patients with suspected right ventricular infarction and patients with chronic lung disease.

Shunt studies

The commonest left to right shunts are ventricular septal defect, atrial septal defect and patent ductus arteriosus. Although the initial assessment of children with congenital heart disease is by echocardiography, the cardiac anatomy may be difficult to define and in these instances first-pass ventriculography may be helpful. Data acquisition is as described above except that gating to the electrocardiogram is not required and a frame rate of 2 frames/s is typically used. There is no need to identify systole and diastole in these studies.

Left to right shunts Regions of interest are placed over the lungs and the aorta and time-activity curves are generated. In the absence of a shunt there is an early rapid increase in radioactivity as the bolus passes through the lungs. This peak falls rapidly and is followed by a second broad peak as the radionuclide recirculates to the heart from the systemic veins. Where there is a shunt, the tracer recirculates early and a second peak occurs, the size of which is proportional to the size of the shunt. The area under the first peak (A1) is proportional to pulmonary blood flow (Qp). The area under the second peak (A2) is proportional to flow through the left to right shunt, which is equal to the difference between the pulmonary and systemic circulations (Qp-Qs). The systemic blood flow is therefore equal to A1-A2. Provided there is no right to left shunt, Qp/Qs can be calculated as A1/(A1-A2).

Normally this ratio is approximately 1. This method is sensitive for detecting a Qp/Qs of between 1.3 and 3. Whilst shunts smaller than this are not detectable, these are clinically insignificant. Larger shunts may be more difficult to quantify, because of persistent high pulmonary activity and poor visualisation of the left ventricle. False-positive diagnoses can occur with coexistent valvular disease and heart failure which cause venous congestion. A bidirectional shunt spuriously reduces the magnitude of the left to right shunt.

Right to left shunts Right to left shunts are usually detected using Doppler echocardiography, radionuclide studies having only a limited role. A right to left shunt is detected by the early appearance of activity in the left heart chambers or the aorta. In a normal first-pass study activity should not be detected in the aorta until after the pulmonary phase of the study. Analysis of the time-activity curve over the aorta can be used to measure the size of a right to left shunt.

Alternatively, right to left shunts can be detected by injecting ^{99m}Tc-macroaggregated albumin, a tracer used mainly in perfusion lung scans, which consists of small particles that are normally trapped within the pulmonary bed. In the presence of a right to left shunt, the pulmonary capillary system is bypassed and the particles enter the arterial circulation, where they are trapped in organs such as the brain and kidneys. The particles are sufficiently small in size and number that there are no clinical sequelae to this embolisation.

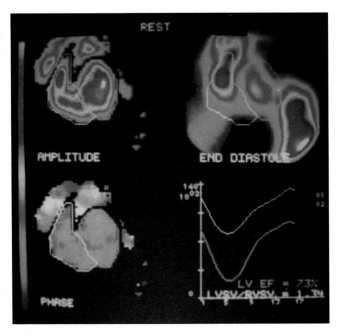

Fig. 1. *Normal radionuclide ventriculography. The panel is divided into 4 quadrants with the smoothed raw counts image top right. Note the rainbow colour scale used for the examples of radionuclide ventriculography. This is shown on the extreme left with low values in light blue and high values in red. This shows a region of interest drawn around the right ventricle with the left ventricle adjacent to it (in green and yellow). Below the left ventricle is high counts from the splenic blood pool (mainly in red). The amplitude and phase values for changes in pixel counts throughout the cardiac cycle are shown on the left side at top and bottom respectively. For the left ventricle the amplitude values are evenly distributed and are all high (showing red) and therefore regional contraction can be seen to be normal. The right ventricular counts (within the region of interest) are also high and normal. In the phase image, the early systolic contraction of both ventricles is depicted in light blue with some green pixels (the right ventricle is outlined again). These minor variations are normal. Note, however, the atrial phase values which are very high (red and pink), as peak contraction occurs late in the cardiac cycle in diastole. The phase difference clearly depicts the atrioventricular valve plane and shows how caudal tilt of the camera is effective in separating left atrial and ventricular counts. The ventricular volume curves are shown in the right bottom quadrant. The left ventricular curve is below that of the right, partly because of interference from right atrial counts which cannot be effectively separated from right ventricular counts. The left ventricular ejection fraction was 73%. (Images supplied by Dr SR Underwood)*

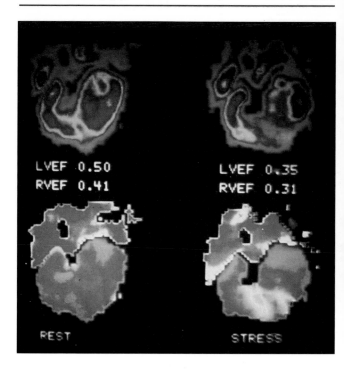

Fig. 2. *Fall in ejection fraction with stress in coronary artery disease. Four images are shown, with the top row representing amplitude and the bottom row phase of contraction of the left ventricle. At rest, in this patient with coronary artery disease, the amplitude and phase images were normal and the left ventricular ejection fraction was 50%. During exercise, however, a large amplitude and phase abnormality occurs in the anterior wall, septum and apex (reduced amplitude of contraction which is delayed in the cardiac cycle) and the ejection fraction fell to 35%. This response indicates very significant myocardial ischaemia. (Images supplied by Dr SR Underwood)*

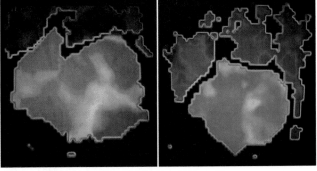

Fig. 3. *Left ventricular aneurysm phase images. The pre-operative phase image is shown on the left. There is an obvious area of dyskinesia in the left ventricular apex which is coloured red. This occurs because pixel counts in this area actually increase in systole whilst the counts elsewhere in the ventricle are decreasing. After resection of the aneurysm, the phase map shows normal ventricular contraction. (Images supplied by Dr SR Underwood)*

References

1. Wackers FJ, Berger HJ, Johnstone DE, et al. Multiple gated cardiac blood pool imaging for left ventricular ejection fraction: validation of the technique and assessment of variability. *Am J Cardiol* 1979; **43**: 1159-65.

2. Hecht HS, Josephson MA, Hopkins JM, Singh BN, Parzen E, Elashoff J. Reproducibility of equilibrium radionuclide ventriculography in patients with coronary artery disease: response of left ventricular ejection fraction and regional wall motion to supine bicycle exercise. *Am Heart J* 1982; **104**: 567-74.

3. Himelman RB, Cassidy MM, Landzberg JS, Schiller NB. Reproducibility of quantitative two-dimensional echocardiography. *Am Heart J* 1988; **115**: 425-31.

4. Ritchie JL, Cerqueira M, Maynard C, David K, Kennedy JW. Ventricular function and infarct size: the Western Washington intravenous streptokinase in myocardial infarction trial. *J Am Coll Cardiol* 1988; **11**: 689-97.

5. Morgan CD, Roberts R, Haw A, et al. Coronary patency, infarct size and left ventricular function after thrombolytic

therapy for acute myocardial infarction: results from the tissue plasminogen activator: Toronto (TPAT) placebo controlled trial. *J Am Coll Cardiol* 1991; **17**: 1451-7.

6. Waagstein F, Bristow MR, Swedberg K, et al. Beneficial effects of metoprolol in idiopathic dilated cardiomyopathy. *Lancet* 1993; **342**: 1441-6.

7. Pfeffer MA, Braunwald E, Moye LA, et al. Effect of captopril on mortality and morbidity in patients with left ventricular dysfunction after myocardial infarction. *N Engl J Med* 1992; **327**: 669-77.

8. DeFeyter PJ, Van Eegenie MJ, Dighton DH, Visser FC, De Jong J, Roos JP. Prognosis value of exercise testing, coronary angiography and left ventriculography 6 to 8 weeks after myocardial infarction. *Circulation* 1982; **66**: 527-36.

9. The Multicentre Postinfarction Research Group. Risk stratification and survival after myocardial infarction. *N Engl J Med* 1983; **309**: 331-6.

10. Pfeffer MA, Braunwald E, Moye LA, et al. Effect of captopril on mortality and morbidity of survivors of acute myocardial infarction – results of the survival and ventricular enlargement trial. *N Engl J Med* 1992; **327**: 669-77.

11. The Acute Infarction Ramipril Efficacy (AIRE) study investigators. Effect of ramipril on mortality and morbidity of survivors of acute myocardial infarction with clinical evidence of heart failure. *Lancet* 1993; **342**: 821-8.

12. Rehani MM, Sharma SK. Site of Tc-99m binding to the red blood cell. *J Nucl Med* 1980; **21**: 676-8.

13. Pavel DG, Zimmer AM, Patterson VN. In vivo labelling of red blood cells with Tc-99m: a new approach to blood pool visualisation. *J Nucl Med* 1977; **18**: 305-8.

14. Prvulovich E, Syed GMS, Underwood SR, Jewitt DE. Improved assessment of inferior left ventricular wall using biplane equilibrium radionuclide ventriculography. *Eur J Nucl Med* 1994; **21**: 423-6.

15. Yiannikas J, MacIntyre WJ, Underwood DA, et al. Prediction of improvement in left ventricular function after ventricular aneurysmectomy using Fourier phase and amplitude imaging of radionuclide cardiac blood pool scans. *Am J Cardiol* 1985; **55**: 1308-12.

Infarct-avid Imaging

INTRODUCTION

Patients with typical myocardial infarction present with chest pain, electrocardiographic changes and a rise in creatine kinase. In these cases myocardial infarction can be diagnosed without recourse to radionuclide imaging, but there are a number of circumstances in which the clinical situation is more difficult, and an independent means of verifying the diagnosis is then helpful. This might occur, for example (a) in patients with pacemakers or conduction abnormalities such as left bundle branch block; (b) after coronary artery grafting, when creatine kinase levels may be elevated; and (c) in patients presenting late after myocardial infarction, when creatine kinase levels may be normal with non-diagnostic electrocardiographic changes.

RADIOPHARMACEUTICALS

Two different radionuclide techniques can be used in the diagnosis of acute myocardial infarction. If a tracer has a high affinity for necrotic tissue, the infarct will appear as a hot area. If a tracer distributes according to perfusion and cell integrity, then the infarct will appear as a cold area, when compared to normal. The two infarct avid tracers are ^{99m}Tc–pyrophosphate and ^{111}In-antimyosin antibodies. A newer agent is currently under evaluation for clinical licensing, namely antimyosin antibodies labelled with ^{99m}Tc. ^{201}Tl and the ^{99m}Tc agents, MIBI and tetrofosmin, are the commonly used myocardial perfusion tracers, but it is difficult to distinguish old from acute infection by perfusion imaging alone.

ANTIMYOSIN ANTIBODIES

Antimyosin antibody is a monoclonal antibody produced by immunising mice with human myosin. Splenic lymphocytes producing the desired antibody are fused with myeloma cells to form hybridomas which produce large quantities of the desired monoclonal antibody. Fab fragments are produced by digesting the whole antibody with papain, pepsin or other chemical agents.

Mechanism of uptake

When ischaemia results in irreversible damage to the cell membrane, myosin is exposed. Myosin is a protein in the myocardial cell membrane with a high molecular weight and low solubility which therefore largely remains fixed when the cell membrane is disrupted. In patients with acute myocardial infarction, antimyosin antibody reaches the infarction via a reperfused artery or collateral vessels. Antimyosin antibodies only bind to irreversibly injured myocardial cells and binding therefore indicates cellular death.[1] Antimyosin antibodies are incorporated into necrotic myocardium with uptake inversely related to regional flow, such that highest uptake is seen in areas with severely impaired coronary flow such as central areas of infarction. Comparisons of infarct size in animals between ^{111}In-antimyosin and histological staining have shown very close correlation.

Radiopharmaceutical

[111]In-antimyosin is the more expensive of the infarct-avid agents and it is associated with the higher radiation burden because of its longer half-life and biodistribution. Currently ^{111}In-antimyosin antibody imaging is not recognised for routine clinical use by ARSAC in the UK, and research studies may only be performed if an ARSAC license is gained. Antimyosin antibody is bound to DTPA to facilitate labelling with ^{111}In, the labelling procedure itself being straightforward. Antimyosin antibody (0.5 mg) labelled with 74 MBq of ^{111}In is administered by slow intravenous injection and the effective dose equivalent is 10.5 mSv.

Skin testing

Administration of antimyosin antibodies to a patient who already has circulating human antimouse antibodies could theoretically provoke either a local or a systemic immune response, and routine skin testing is therefore recommended. A small dose of labelled antibody (0.01 ml) is injected intradermally and if no skin wheal is noted after 30 min, antibody can be injected with a low risk of allergic reactions.

Timing of studies

Studies should not be performed earlier than 24 h after suspected infarction to allow time for re-establishment of blood flow. Within approximately 10-14 days of infarction the replacement of damaged myocytes by fibrous tissue begins, myosin disappears and antimyosin antibody uptake within areas of infarction fades. In some patients persistent antimyosin uptake is seen several weeks to months after myocardial infarction because of slow clearance of the large myosin molecule by granulocytes.

Data acquisition

Typical acquisition parameters are shown in Table 1. Images are acquired with the patient supine and the left arm positioned above the head. Planar images are usually acquired in three projections, but tomographic acquisition is possible. Optimal imaging for infarction is at 48 h after injection because of persistent high blood pool activity, but 24-h imaging can be attempted, and if this is positive, further delay can be avoided. The 67-h half-life of ^{111}In allows imaging up to 3 days after injection if necessary.

Normal images

In the absence of necrosis, the images reflect the normal biodistribution of antimyosin antibody with renal, liver, spleen and bone marrow uptake.

Medium-energy collimator
128 x 128 matrix
20% windows at 171 and 245 keV
Anterior, left anterior oblique and left lateral views
500 kcounts per view
Optimal imaging 48 h after injection
Optimal timing typically 1-10 days after symptom onset

Table 1 *Typical imaging parameters for ^{111}In-antimyosin imaging*

Image analysis

If there is myocardial necrosis, abnormal cardiac uptake is present. Subjective interpretation of images is possible if myocardial uptake of ^{111}In-antimyosin antibody is compared to lung uptake. Quantitative analysis is also possible.

Sensitivity and specificity

The sensitivity of this technique for Q wave infarction is >90% in all reported series. For non-Q wave infarction, there is a sensitivity of 78%-84%. The intensity of uptake and the proportion of positive results is higher in anterior than in inferior infarction, owing to the relative distance of these regions from the camera and physiological liver activity. The specificity of the technique ranges from 85% to 90%. Uptake may also be seen in unstable angina, which reflects patchy necrosis only.[2]

^{99m}Tc-Antimyosin

The ^{99m}Tc-antimyosin tracer is not yet available for clinical studies but is currently under investigation. Early studies show good detection rates for acute infarction. This tracer has the advantages of availability, simple reconstitution in 30 min and imaging of infarction within 6-8 h after injection. The images are of high quality because of the significantly higher injected

dose (up to 1000 MBq has been used) which is possible with
the shorter half-life of ^{99m}Tc. The initial blood pool activity
also allows ventriculography to be performed with the
same dose.

^{99M}Tc-PYROPHOSPHATE

^{99m}Tc-pyrophosphate was originally developed as a bone
scanning agent but has also been used for infarct detection.
In areas of myocardial necrosis, calcium phosphate is deposited.

Mechanism of uptake

Two factors limit the time window for ^{99m}Tc-pyrophosphate
imaging in the diagnosis of myocardial infarction: there must
be adequate arterial delivery of the tracer to the area of
infarction, and adequate calcium in the necrotic cells for
binding. Arterial reperfusion in the absence of thrombolysis
requires 12-24 h, and the deposition of calcium is also time
dependent, being low during an episode of ischaemia and
gradually increasing.

Delivery of ^{99m}Tc-pyrophosphate is greatest to myocardial
areas with a reduction of blood flow to 20%-40% of normal.
Regions with very low blood supply fail to demonstrate
significant tracer uptake and in large areas of infarction
therefore, uptake is often absent centrally with significant
peripheral tracer uptake. This gives rise to a "doughnut"
pattern of tracer uptake. Comparison of infarct size by
pyrophosphate imaging with histology in animals suggests that
pyrophosphate overestimates infarct size.

Radiopharmaceutical

Chromatography is performed to ensure low levels of free
pertechnetate which would remain within the blood pool
and interfere with cardiac imaging. Up to 600 MBq
^{99m}Tc-pyrophosphate is injected intravenously at rest.
The effective dose equivalent is less than 5 mSv.

Timing of studies

Studies should not be performed earlier than 24 h after suspected infarction. At this time blood flow should be re-established and calcium is present in the infarct area. Removal of necrotic myocytes proceeds rapidly after infarction and within 5-7 days inadequate amounts of calcium are available for binding. Optimal imaging is therefore between 2 and 5 days after symptom onset.

Data acquisition

Typical acquisition parameters are shown in Table 2.
No patient preparation is required. Images are acquired with the patient supine and the left arm above the head. Imaging is performed 2-6 hours after injection to allow clearance of the majority of the tracer from the blood pool. Waiting longer allows additional clearance of blood pool and soft tissue activity, but reduces counts from the infarct area.
Planar images are taken in three projections, and tomographic imaging is also possible.

Normal images

Normal images delineate the bony structures of the thorax with no tracer activity in the region of the myocardium.

Low-energy, high-resolution collimator
128 x 128 matrix
20% window at 140 keV
Anterior, left anterior oblique and left lateral views
500 kcounts per view
Optimal imaging 2-6 h after injection
Optimal timing typically 2-5 days after symptom onset

Table 2 *Typical imaging parameters for ^{99m}Tc-pyrophosphate imaging*

Image analysis

The interpretation of cardiac images in myocardial infarction is based on the analysis of intensity and localisation of uptake in the thorax. Uptake intensity is usually graded from 1 to 4 when compared with normal bone uptake. The spine and sternum are taken as reference points. Difficulties in interpretation are encountered when uptake follows the distribution of activity in either the ribs or the costal cartilages. Software techniques to correct for rib activity on planar images are difficult. Tomography avoids myocardial overlap by overlying bony structures and the target to background ratio, sensitivity and ease of image interpretation are improved.

Sensitivity and specificity

The sensitivity and specificity of ^{99m}Tc-pyrophosphate imaging for infarct detection varies considerably in the literature. False-negative studies occur if imaging is performed too early or too late, or if reperfusion or collateralisation is poor.

Imaging with ^{99m}Tc-pyrophosphate is 90%-96% sensitive for full-thickness anterior infarction. Sensitivity for small, inferior or subendocardial infarcts is much lower. The specificity of the study is 60%-80% depending on the presence or absence of other cardiac conditions that may lead to pyrophosphate accumulation over the cardiac area. Some of the many causes of such false-positive studies are shown in Table 3. In unstable angina tracer uptake may be seen which may reflect prior or ongoing myocardial ischaemia or necrosis. In addition, patients with old myocardial infarcts may continue to have positive myocardial uptake of ^{99m}Tc-pyrophosphate over extended periods. In one study 18%-57% of patients showed persistent tracer uptake months or years after infarction, due possibly to the presence of non-reabsorbed calcium complexes in the infarcted area.

Unstable angina
Ventricular aneurysm
Recent electrical cardioversion
Valve calcification
Pericarditis
Myocarditis
Amyloidosis
Previous myocardial infarction

Table 3 *Causes of false-positive ^{99m}Tc-pyrophosphate images for acute infarction*

THALLIUM-201

Uptake mechanism

Thallium-201 is taken up by myocardial cells with normal cellular membrane integrity in proportion to regional blood flow.

Data acquisition

Studies can be performed using either planar or tomographic imaging. Tomography is more sensitive but requires the patient to be moved away from the coronary care unit whilst planar imaging can be performed at the bedside.

Image analysis

When injected at rest, areas of infarcted myocardium appear as cold spots in the myocardial image. In patients with chest pain, serial imaging can be used to differentiate ischaemia in which redistribution occurs, from myocardial infarction in which the defect is persistent. Thallium imaging cannot distinguish between old and new infarction.

Sensitivity and specificity

The acquisition of thallium myocardial perfusion images is covered elsewhere. The sensitivity of thallium rest–redistribution studies for detection of significant Q wave infarction is very high.

OTHER APPLICATIONS OF ANTIMYOSIN ANTIBODY IMAGING

Diagnosis of cardiac transplant rejection

Allograft rejection accounts for almost a third of mortality after cardiac transplantation. Clear evidence of rejection is required before treatment with high-dose immunosuppressive therapy is started because of the side-effects. Although right ventricular biopsy is the gold standard for detecting and monitoring transplant rejection, this is a costly and invasive procedure. Furthermore, as only a few myocardial areas are biopsied, rejection may be missed. An inexpensive, non–invasive method of assessing the entire heart for rejection would therefore be useful.

In a comparative study of ^{111}In-antimyosin and cardiac biopsy, antimyosin antibody was 94% sensitive and 28% specific for moderate to severe transplant rejection seen on biopsy.[3] The low specificity may have been due to the sampling error associated with cardiac biopsy or the continuing presence of residual necrotic myocytes after a rejection episode. In another study, patients were studied every 4 months with antimyosin antibody and 67% of patients with a heart lung-ratio of 1.55 and 80% of patients with a heart-lung ratio greater than 1.75 experienced a subsequent episode of rejection.[4]

Diagnosis of myocarditis

When a young patient presents with fever and elevated erythrocyte sedimentation rate, white cell count and creatine kinase with progression to cardiac failure, the diagnosis of myocarditis may be straightforward. However, in many patients presenting with dilated cardiomyopathy the aetiology is unclear. Cardiac biopsy can be performed but the findings are often non-specific and areas of myocarditis may be missed. Antimyosin antibody has been used in these circumstances to aid diagnosis. In one study antimyosin antibody imaging had a 100% sensitivity and 58% specificity for myocarditis compared with myocardial biopsy.[5] In another, abnormal uptake of antimyosin antibody was found in 55% of patients with suspected myocarditis who underwent endomyocardial biopsy. Six-month follow-up showed spontaneous improvement in 54% of patients with positive scans and negative biopsies consistent with the clinical course of myocarditis.[6] A high prevalence of abnormal uptake has also been observed in chronic idiopathic dilated cardiomyopathy.[7]

Cardiotoxicity

Uptake of antimyosin antibodies in patients treated with chemotherapy may be a possible marker of myocardial damage.[8] Uptake can be detected before there is deterioration of left ventricular systolic function.

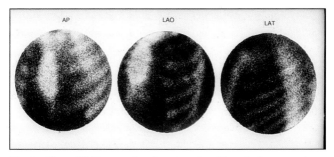

Fig. 1. Normal ^{99m}Tc-pyrophosphate imaging. Note the bone uptake which is normal. The sternum and ribs are clearly seen in the anteroposterior (AP), left anterior oblique (LAO) and lateral (LAT) views

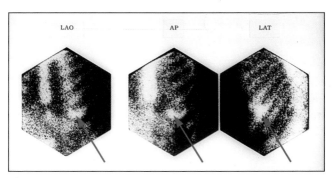

Fig. 2. Inferior myocardial infarction detection with ^{99m}Tc–pyrophosphate. In addition to bone uptake there is now activity in the inferior wall of the heart. This is seen in all three views and is suggestive of inferior infarction

References

1. Khaw BA, Scott J, Fallon JT, et al. Myocardial injury: quantitation by cell sorting initiated with antimyosin flourescent spheres. *Science* 1982; **217**: 1050-.

2. Jain D, Lahiri A, Raval U, et al. Extent of subclinical myocardial necrosis in patients with unstable angina detected by indium-111 antimyosin antibody imaging. *Br Heart J* 1988; **59**: 631.

3. Ballaster Rodes M, Carrio-Gasset I, Abadal-Berini L, et al. Patterns of evolution of myocyte damage after human heart transplantation detected by indium-111 monoclonal antimyosin. *Am J Cardiol* 1988; **62**: 623-27.

4. Ballaster M, Obrador D, Carrio I, et al. Indium-111 monoclonal antimyosin antibody studies after the first year of heart transplantation: identification of risk groups for developing rejection during long-term follow-up and clinical implications. *Circulation* 1990; **82**: 2100-8.

5. Yasuda T, Palacaios I, Dec G, et al. Indium-111 monoclonal antimyosin antibody imaging in the diagnosis of acute myocarditis. *Circulation* 1987; **76**: 306-11.

6. Dec GW, Palacios I, Yasuda T, et al. Antimyosin antibody cardiac imaging: its role in the diagnosis of myocarditis. *J Am Coll Cardiol* 1990; **16**: 97-104.

7. Obrador D, Ballester M, Carrio I, Berna L, Pon-Llado G. High prevalence of myocardial monoclonal antimyosin antibody uptake in patients with chronic idiopathic dilated cardiomyopathy. *J Am Coll Cardiol* 1989; **13**: 1289-93.

8. Lee MC, LaFrance ND, Takeda K, et al. Indium-111 antimyosin monoclonal antibody in the detection of doxorubicin induced cardiotoxicity. *Nuklearmedizin* 1986: **25**: A40.

Positron Emission Tomography

INTRODUCTION

Like gamma emitters, positron emitters can be used to label tracers. These radionuclides decay with emission of a positron, which is a positively charged particle with the same mass as an electron. The emitted positrons travel a short distance from the originating nucleus before taking part in an annihilation reaction with an electron. This results in the generation of two 511 keV gamma photons travelling in opposite directions. Positron emission tomography (PET) is based on the detection of these two gamma photons. Series of detectors are placed in rings around the patient's body, and an event is only registered when gamma photons are recorded simultaneously in two opposite detectors, a method known as coincidence detection. Localisation of the site of the original radioactive photon is possible to within the distance the positron travelled prior to annihilation. Tomographic images are produced using standard backprojection reconstruction techniques to estimate the coordinates of the annihilation events detected by the various 180° opposed detectors.

For attenuation correction to be possible a transmission scan must be acquired before each patient study. Events from a continuous ring source of gadolinium or other long-lived source are recorded with the patient inside (transmission scan) and outside the detector field of view (blank scan). The attenuation correction factor is simply the ratio of transmission scan to blank scan events.

ADVANTAGES OF PET COMPARED TO SPET

There are a number of advantages of PET over single-photon emission tomography (SPET) (Table 1). Naturally occurring biological molecules such as isotopes of carbon, nitrogen and oxygen can be used as tracers. The short half-lives of most positron emitters mean that the radiation dose to the patient is kept to a minimum and allows studies at rest or after stress to be performed within reasonably short periods. The use of higher energy gamma rays leads to reduced photon attenuation, improved spatial resolution compared to SPET (4-8 mm versus 10 mm for cardiac studies) and higher sensitivity. PET is able to remove the effect of attenuation with depth and as a result greater accuracy in the measurement of regional activity is possible and assessments of absolute tracer concentration may be made using appropriate kinetic models.

Advantages

    Naturally occurring biological molecules can be labelled

    Attenuation correction is routinely performed

    Improved spatial resolution

    Improved sensitivity

    Calculation of organ tracer concentration possible

    Low radiation dosimetry

    Studies may be repeated over short time intervals

Disadvantages

    A cyclotron is needed on site of nearby

    High expense

    High level of on-site expertise

    Labelling and quality control must be performed rapidly

    Currently limited clinical application in the heart

    Dynamic exercise not easily performed with studies

Table 1 *PET compared with SPET*

DISADVANTAGES OF PET COMPARED TO SPET

There are, however, a number of disadvantages of PET compared to SPET (Table 1). Most positron emitters are cyclotron produced and have short half-lives (less than 2 h). The short half-life means that production must be close to the site of use and that labelling and quality control must be performed quickly. The high gamma photon energy requires large amounts of lead shielding and makes imaging using conventional gamma cameras difficult both because the crystal is not thick enough for efficient detection and because scattered photons cause unacceptable image degradation. Claustrophobia is a problem for some patients lying within the ring of detectors. Imaging protocols can be very lengthy and it is difficult to couple dynamic exercise with PET. Finally, costs of PET are high because of the need for cyclotron radiotracer production and complex imaging equipment. Typically a PET study for myocardial viability costs £800-1000.

MYOCARDIAL BLOOD FLOW STUDIES

The most commonly used agents for evaluating myocardial blood flow are ^{13}N-ammonia, ^{15}O-water and ^{82}Rb.

Rubidium-82 ^{82}Rb is a potassium analogue which is generator produced. Energy is required for its transportation into the myocardial cell via the Na^+-K^+ pump. Its physical half-life is 76 s and images must therefore be acquired quickly after injection. Myocardial uptake of ^{82}Rb is linearly related to blood flow except at the high rates of blood flow, when flow is underestimated. Consecutive imaging at rest and after pharmacological stress is possible within 10 min of one another.

^{13}N-ammonia This tracer is cyclotron produced and has a physical half-life of 10 min. Tracer is avidly extracted by myocardial tissue and retained in the form of glutamine.

Myocardial uptake of ^{13}N-ammonia is linearly related to blood flow except at high flow rates, when flow is underestimated. Consecutive imaging at rest and after pharmacological stress is feasible within 60-90 min of one another. Good-quality images are produced with high contrast between heart and surrounding lung and blood pool activity. Liver uptake can impair evaluation of the inferior wall.

^{15}O-water ^{15}O-water is cyclotron produced and has a physical half-life of 20 s. It diffuses rapidly across the myocardial membrane, but the residual time in the cell is short and it quickly equilibrates between tissue and the intravascular space. Myocardial uptake is linearly related to blood flow at even the highest rates of blood flow, but stringent imaging requirements and the need for a separate PET study for blood pool subtraction mean that it is the least commonly used of the blood flow tracers.

STUDY OF MYOCARDIAL METABOLISM

When there is adequate blood flow and oxygen supply, the primary substrate for ATP production is fatty acids. If blood flow and oxygen supply become reduced, myocardial cells switch to anaerobic glycolysis for ATP production, and in infarcted areas no glycolysis occurs. ^{18}F-Fluorodeoxyglucose (FDG) is a glucose analogue, is transported into the myocyte by the same carrier as glucose, has a half-life of 110 min and is cyclotron produced. Imaging with ^{18}F-FDG requires strict control of blood glucose levels, as in hypoglycaemic states myocardial metabolism is preferentially shifted away from glycolysis.

INDICATIONS FOR CARDIAC POSITRON EMISSION TOMOGRAPHY

Positron emission tomography has a sensitivity of >90% for the identification of coronary artery disease, which in general is higher than by SPET thallium perfusion imaging.[1] Although PET has slightly higher sensitivity, there is no justification for the routine use of PET in the investigation of cardiac patients. The only true indication for cardiac PET studies is the identification of hibernating myocardium before revascularisation, but approximately 90% of cases will be identified by thallium imaging using a resting injection, and PET is often only used in difficult cases.

IMAGING PROTOCOL FOR MYOCARDIAL HIBERNATION

The imaging protocol for myocardial hibernation typically involves rest ^{13}N-ammonia imaging (250 MBq) followed by stress ^{13}N-ammonia (250 MBq) imaging, and finally rest ^{18}F–FDG imaging (550 MBq). Most departments perform some form of "glucose clamp" in an attempt to improve the quality of ^{18}F-FDG images. Typically, on arrival in the department the patient's blood sugar is measured. If this is less than 8 g/dl, 50 g of glucose is given intravenously. At the end of the ^{13}N-ammonia sequence the patient's blood sugar is again measured. At this stage insulin is given according to a sliding scale depending on the blood sugar level.

Each of the ^{13}N-ammonia images takes 20-25 min to acquire and pharmacological stress takes 10 min. ^{18}F-FDG can be injected immediately afterwards but imaging should not begin until 30 min after injection and takes 20 min. Therefore the imaging protocol takes just under 2 h to complete.

IDENTIFICATION OF HIBERNATING MYOCARDIUM USING CARDIAC PET

Areas of hibernating myocardium typically have increased ^{18}F–FDG uptake but reduced perfusion as demonstrated by ^{13}N–ammonia or [82]Rb studies. By contrast areas of fibrotic myocardium typically have reduced perfusion and reduced ^{18}F–FDG uptake. The finding of decreased flow and increased glucose metabolism is an accurate way of distinguishing hibernating myocardium from myocardial fibrosis, with positive and negative predictive values of approximately 85% for identifying regions that will improve after revascularisation.[2]

The identification of hibernating myocardium by PET has been shown to be predictive of improved global left ventricular ejection fraction,[2] improved heart failure symptoms[3] and improved survival after revascularisation.[4]

References

1. Rozanski A, Berman DS. The efficacy of cardiovascular nuclear medicine studies. *Semin Nucl Med* 1987; **17:** 104-20.
2. Tillisch JH, Brunken R, Marshall R, Schwaiger M, Mandelkorn M, Phelps M, Schelbert H. Reversibility of cardiac wall motion abnormalities predicted by positron emission tomography. *N Engl J Med* 1986; **314:** 884-8.
3. DiCarli M, Khanna S, Davidson M, et al. The value of PET for predicting improvement in heart failure symptoms in patients with coronary disease and severe left ventricular dysfunction. *J Am Coll Cardiol* 1993; **21:** 129A.
4. Eitzman D, Al-Aouar Z, Kanter HL, et al. Clinical outcome of patients with coronary artery disease after viability studies with positron emission tomography. *J Am Coll Cardiol* 1992; **20:** 550-65.